IN EACH OTHER'S BONES

A MEMOIR OF LOVE, LOSS, AND LIVING

JULIA FREIFELD

I dedicate this book to my grandchildren: Noah Mark, Elise Mira, Max Chandler, and Maya Ruth. Each of you has the blessing of being named after your Grandpa Mark.
Keep him in your hearts.

Instead of wondering why bad things are allowed to happen, consider instead that there are no "good" or "bad" things in the universe, only creations that move us forward in our evolution. We cannot judge these creations, because they are necessary in order for growth and expansion to occur. They are there to provide traction, something to push against, like a swimmer pushing off the edge of a pool.

—TERRI DANIEL
*Embracing Death: A New Look at Grief,
Gratitude and God*

Someday,
when I'm awfully low
and the world is cold
I will feel a glow
just thinking of you

—"THE WAY YOU LOOK TONIGHT"
BY DOROTHY FIELDS AND JEROME KERN

CONTENTS

Prologue

FOR TEN YEARS, MY BELOVED husband, Mark, battled a rare, terminal neurological disease. For those ten years, fear was constantly exploding inside me. I feared losing him, feared our family dynamic would change, and feared losing my sense of self. I realized I had to change my focus away from fear in order to survive. I was not willing to be a victim.

I wanted to remain Mark's wife and not solely his nurse. The strength of our marriage was in place before Mark's disease, multiple system atrophy (MSA), entered our lives. From the very beginning, we were hand in hand, being gentle with each other as the symptoms piled up and our hearts were broken bit by precious bit. Through this process, Mark and I redefined what love and marriage look like.

I grasped for something solid within myself. It was the hardest thing I'd ever done. Mark's illness began a spiritual journey for me. Through the use of ritual, creativity, and nature, I maintained a connection to life. I lived openly, fully, and emotionally. I learned to hunt for joy while being handed plates full of sadness.

It was a journey within myself but not by myself. Many people became teachers for me during this unfamiliar journey. Family and friends were a chain of love. They surrounded and sustained me.

Toward the end, I felt battered by loss as I watched my wonderful husband of thirty-two years submit to this horrendous disease. MSA robbed me of Mark. I struggled to get through this chapter of my life with the least amount of damage and stay whole. Sometimes I failed. Sometimes I flourished.

My book summarizes almost fourteen years of my life: the ten years from the beginning of Mark's illness to his dying and the four years that followed. I wrote on and off over those years. After Mark's death, I wrote on anything I could find: napkins, scraps of paper, sticky notes, backs of receipts, envelopes, sheets torn out of a calendar or pulled from a notebook. Later, I assembled the hundreds of bits of paper, lined them up by date on the floor, and began typing into my computer again. Writing helped me pick up the crumbling pieces of our life together and make sense of this senselessness.

My book is a love letter, a Valentine card, and a thank-you note all rolled into one for Mark. I want to return all the love he gave me. It is odd to write an entire book about Mark's illness and dying when he loved everything about life and living. When he woke up each morning, his first words were "Let's go!" Mark loved fixing a plumbing leak, coaching his children's sports teams, chatting with the mailman. He loved people—family, friends, strangers—and people loved Mark. I could always find Mark at a party; people were usually circled around him laughing.

Though this love letter is marred with bruises, ripped hearts, and tears, it is still a love letter, perhaps more real and lifelike for all that. In the end, there was only love, not resentment.

I have included my paintings, poems, and dreams in the book because these are as much about who I am and what I experienced as the words I have written. I know my paintings will be different in the future. My poems were like dreams, and my dreams were like guides.

I will dream about Mark forever.

Family photo at Laguna Beach, California, 2004.
Top row: David, Jeremy, Emily. Mark and me in front.

EARLY STAGE:
QUESTIONS AND DOUBTS

CHAPTER ONE

Moving Toward a Diagnosis

THERE IS A PARALLEL UNIVERSE. Seen in clear sunlight are the healthy. Existing behind hospital and home walls are people with chronic illnesses and diseases of all sorts. Their families, often at wits' end, hang by a thread beside them.

My husband, Mark, began exhibiting early symptoms of multiple system atrophy (MSA) in 2004 when we were both forty-eight years old. We had three children: Jeremy was twenty years old and a junior in college, Emily was eighteen and a freshman in college, and David was thirteen and in middle school. We were a young family, too young to think about retiring, too young to think about dying.

When the disease entered our lives, I had never experienced such hardship and loss. I had lost grandparents, elderly relatives, and distant friends, but suddenly I was confronting the largest loss of all: my husband. There were no baby steps to prepare me for what was ahead. Every day and every doctor's appointment was just one more giant plunge into the darkest and saddest kind of grief.

Mark's first symptoms were dizziness and lightheadedness, which we learned were the result of abnormally low blood pressure, or orthostatic hypotension.[1] He had bladder issues as well. In 2004, we walked into Mark's first neurological appointment looking for answers and a cure for what was happening to him. From 2004 to 2011, Mark met with thirteen neurologists, along with urologists, gastroenterologists, and movement disorder specialists.

In 2007, based on his ongoing orthostatic hypotension, he was referred to a neurologist at the Lahey Clinic in Boston who specialized in autonomic dysfunction.[2] After several tests, the doctor believed Mark's illness was indeed autonomic dysfunction, which has no cure but is not fatal. Her prognosis: Mark could live a long time with few other complications.

But new symptoms arose, and our worries kept gnawing at us. In 2008, he saw a neuro-urologist at the Medical Center at Emory University in Atlanta. This doctor was certain Mark had occult spinal dysraphism.[3] Like autonomic dysfunction, this was a disease that wasn't fatal. Unfortunately, after a short time and more investigation and testing, Mark learned he did not have occult spinal dysraphism.

Another time, a young neurology intern stepped into the exam room with a big smile. He was tall and lanky and looked about fifteen years old. He wore the same style loafers as our younger son, David. The intern was there to take Mark's history. Mark answered the questions in a straightforward manner. Slowly, as the answers became more complex, as well as the symptoms, the young intern's face became serious.

---

1 Orthostatic hypotension is abnormally low blood pressure while standing, resulting in lightheadedness, dizziness, and weakness.

2 Autonomic dysfunction impairs the nerves that regulate autonomic body functions such as blood pressure.

3 Occult spinal dysraphism impacts the spine, spinal cord, or nerves.

Several times, the intern looked in my direction. Not knowing what to do or say, I tentatively assumed Mark's confident manner. I felt heartbroken once again, hearing the horrid details of Mark's growing symptoms. When we left, we both felt queasy and drained. Mark was still driving at the time. Although I felt awful, it was my turn to be the stronger one, and I drove home because the meeting had left Mark feeling dizzy.

A typical week for Mark during this time went something like this: Monday: two blood tests; Tuesday: skin cancer check; Wednesday: nerve study test; Thursday: MRI of the brain; Friday: EEG. On good weeks, we had the weekend off. In his memoir, *Reflections*, Mark wrote that he sometimes felt like a complicated math problem the doctors weren't trying hard enough to solve. I felt like they were doing the best they could but didn't have any answers. He hoped I was right.

Throughout all the appointments and tests, Mark continued to search for answers and for the doctor who could cure him. He subjected himself to test after grueling test with his head held high. He never complained. He heard weird news, bad news, and sad news, always hoping to eventually hear the piece of the puzzle that could cure or at least help him understand this horrible condition. Nature felt so cruel in giving him this disease.

During an appointment with his internist, Mark mentioned he felt better with his legs elevated. "Perhaps I should start walking on my hands," he said. It made the doctor laugh.

One doctor told Mark he asked too many questions. Mark told him he should have become a veterinarian so he wouldn't have to endure questions from his patients.

I nicknamed one of the neurologists we saw "Dr. Diva." He breezed in and out of the room with a big smile and advised Mark to "Hang in there!"

What kind of medical advice is that? Fuck! There were a lot of "what the fuck" moments with Mark's doctors. Chronic illness is filled with fucked-up surprises.

As Mark's symptoms progressed, I wondered: How do I go through something like this and remain sane? How do I continue living a full life? How do I not become a burden to others? When and how much do I share with my children? How long will Mark's decline last?

In 2009, during a visit at Duke Integrative Medicine, the kindhearted doctor said Mark had the mother lode of neurological symptoms. We discussed healing versus curing. Healing doesn't remove symptoms; it's a process that includes mental, spiritual, and emotional well-being. Curing is a return to health, a life absent of symptoms. She recounted a time in medical school, during her neurology rotation, when she was first introduced to the varieties of neurological conditions. The information, symptoms, and prognoses were staggering. She naively asked the professor about available treatments for these patients. The professor glibly answered: "No hope, no hurry."

It was becoming clearer there was going to be no cure for Mark. We were beginning to feel our hearts and our hopes sinking. Four years later, by the spring of 2013, Mark would be under the care of hospice.

While writing this book, I found an old notebook with my list of questions to ask the doctors:

- Have you seen patients with symptoms like Mark's?

- Are there any recent cures or discoveries that could give Mark some relief?

- We would like to be part of the solution. Can anything be done? Can you be specific?

- Will exercise create healthy impulses down Mark's neural pathways?

- What is the root of Mark's problem?

- Can you help Mark?

Looking at these questions, I can see the desperation I felt and recall my sadness when there were no answers.

As Mark's condition continued to change, his neurologist at the University of North Carolina at Chapel Hill (UNC–Chapel Hill) mentioned her connections with Mayo Clinic in Rochester, Minnesota. She felt it was time for him to meet with Dr. Phillip Low, the leading expert there on multiple system atrophy.

MSA is a rare, terminal neurodegenerative disorder with no known cause. Previously known as Shy-Drager syndrome, "MSA is an adult-onset disorder characterized by a combination of autonomic dysfunction, Parkinsonism, and a failure of muscular coordination. It is often referred to as "prime of life neurodegeneration." It is on a spectrum of other rare diseases that often afflict people during productive, active years and lead to debilitating symptoms and early death."[4]

Three in a hundred thousand people get it. There is no identifiable cause, research leading to a cure, or way to slow the progression of the disease. MSA develops over seven to twelve years. There is no remission. It is a smoldering process. One doctor said, "MSA is as bad a disease as you can get."

In early 2009, we still hadn't told anyone what was happening. In January of that year, our daughter, Emily, got married to James, and one

---

4 CurePSP, *Prime of Life Brain Diseases,* https://www.psp.org/iwanttolearn/prime-of-life-brain-disease/msa/.

week later, Mark and I flew to Minnesota and met with Dr. Low for the first time. We did not tell anyone we were making the trek to Mayo Clinic. We said it was a business trip.

By this point in our journey, we had heard so many varying medical opinions, and with no real definitive diagnosis, we weren't ready to discuss Mark's physical changes with anyone besides his doctors. Plus, he was still able to work, travel, and go out with friends and family.

By going to Mayo Clinic, we were hoping to get a confirmed diagnosis of some underlying cause, along with a medical protocol to handle the progressing symptoms. During our first meeting with Dr. Low, he confirmed Mark's earlier diagnosis of autonomic dysfunction.

After returning home from that first meeting with Dr. Low, Mark would periodically announce to me: "There are changes." When he said this, he was often referring to even the smallest change his body was making. Whenever he said this, I felt like a thunderbolt struck through to my own nervous system.

I didn't know what to do, where to go, or how to stop what was happening, so I placed a photo on the fridge of a cute elderly couple nose to nose, laughing. I told Mark, "That will be us one day."

Mark's immune system was weakening. By the end of 2009, in addition to having trouble with blood pressure and balance, bladder and gastrointestinal issues, and general fatigue, Mark was diagnosed with tonsil cancer. He began treatment right away: surgery to remove the tonsil and radiation. That same year, Mark had to be rushed to the emergency room by ambulance because of an allergic reaction. He also had a cancerous mole removed.

A year later, we met with Dr. Low for the second time, and he alluded to the possibility Mark might have MSA. Our hearts became heavy as concrete. We left dazed. Our minds felt muddled. We walked the hallways of Mayo Clinic aimlessly, hand in hand, hardly glancing at each other. Mark, who usually liked to make plans, said: "I don't want to know the course of this."

The next day, during another appointment, Dr. Low expressed regret at having brought up the possibility of MSA the day before. He must have seen the terror in our faces. We later learned that, in general, neurologists wait for more symptoms to appear before diagnosing a disease. We returned home to Raleigh under a new cloud. It didn't matter that Dr. Low had backpedaled and apologized. The bomb had hit. We knew.

You always know.

There were times when I remained calm as I listened to facts about MSA and the treatments. I would write down names of doctors and procedures, Google everything on the subject, and then carefully clear all my searches so Mark wouldn't discover how often I was researching MSA and related neurological conditions.

After Dr. Low's slip regarding MSA, the "usual" no longer continued in our life. From that moment on, Mark's chronic illness and its changing ways became the way of our life and the shadow of our future. We began adding assistive equipment to our home and to Mark's daily life. We added grab bars to our bathrooms, and Mark bought his first walking sticks. The arrival of the various pieces of equipment was as much an insult to his ego as they were an aid to his physical failings.

Mark and I decided we wanted a happy home, not a home of tears. Mark said he felt sad when he saw me sad. I couldn't hide my sadness. My entire mouth filled with tears before they appeared in my eyes. I had never cried like this before. I couldn't believe he might have this condition: so rare, no cure, no future.

One night, I left a page in my journal blank. Our future was like a blank page: unformed, unclear, invisible, and unknowable, not like the future we had always planned to have together. I filled another page in my journal with the word "No" written about seventy times. It was *no* to everything deteriorating in Mark's body. When I tried to think about the future, my heart felt smashed to bits. Our time together began to feel like a slow descent into tragedy.

One night, when Mark and I were in bed, we started talking.

Me: "What can I do for you?"

Mark: "Just be you."

Me: "I want you in my life . . . always, in any form."

Mark: "Be careful what you wish for."

CHAPTER TWO

Keeping a Secret

The best way of keeping a secret is to pretend there isn't one.
—MARGARET ATWOOD

AS MARK'S HEALTH CHANGED, he felt he could take care of his health by himself. He believed he could stay ahead of whatever physical problems were cropping up by being informed and connected to doctors who could help. He made a conscious decision to not burden others. He didn't want his illness to be the topic of others' conversations or speculations. It also gave him a feeling of control in his life during a time when he didn't have control. I respected his decision and obliged. Sometimes, keeping a secret with someone is a bonding experience; two people sharing personal matters can feel intimate.

Yet I felt torn. Whose secret was it?

I had to remind myself I wasn't intentionally withholding information. I was guarding Mark's privacy. My promise to Mark was bigger than my bottled-up feelings of worry and fear. Right after going to another specialist and getting another possible diagnosis with another list of symptoms and complications, it was not unusual for me to run into a friend and act as if I didn't have a care in the world. I have asked friends now if they detected anything. They've all said no.

Before we told our children, were they noticing changes in their father? In 2008, while on a family vacation, Emily stumbled upon Mark's catheters. She didn't know what they were and didn't ask any questions. It was years later that she admitted to finding them. Since we held back any explanation, did our children feel betrayed? We raised them to talk things through and tell the truth, but talking about illness and death is tricky. And not everyone is up for those kinds of conversations. I really didn't know how to talk about what was happening.

I have often been other people's secret keeper. Friends and strangers have confided in me my whole life. I am like a vault. Secrets don't leak out, even my own. Mark and I didn't plan on keeping a secret like this for as long as we did. The years crept up on us. Denial is a wonderful thing. It was like a drug I kept trying to swallow.

However, by keeping my feelings locked deep inside, I was allowing them to snowball into something larger. Keeping Mark's secret became harder as every day, every week, every month, things were getting scarier. I was torn between protecting his privacy and releasing my own overburdened emotions. To cope, I began meeting with a therapist. It was the first time I had told anyone what was going on. My therapist and I discussed my need to begin sharing my worries, sadness, and fears with a few select friends.

Shortly after, a friend asked about Mark. I couldn't pretend anymore. I broke down. Everything poured out of me so fast and strong, I couldn't stop talking and crying. My sobs were gigantic. Some words describing Mark's symptoms were so hard to say aloud, I had to whisper them to her. This was the first crack in the dam.

By talking to my therapist and opening myself up to friends, I experienced many difficult yet honest conversations. I was becoming more real with myself and others. My relationships with family and friends deepened and grew, rather than collapsed as I had feared. I was beginning to understand that when we share troubles, we learn the beauty of genuine friendship and are able to make true connections.

When Mark got tonsil cancer, we told our children about his neurological symptoms and doctor visits. Jeremy was twenty-six years old at the time, living in Chapel Hill with his girlfriend, Jenn. Jeremy was working for Mark part-time and was getting ready to start law school. Emily, twenty-four, and James were living in Washington, DC, and she had just begun graduate school for museum education. David was nineteen, a sophomore in college.

Telling our children about the cancer and the neurological symptoms was the beginning of letting them see me not just as a mother, wife, and caregiver but as a human being moving through life with heartache and happiness. I was showing them it can be done. Initially, keeping the secret was like building a small house that just the two of us squeezed into. Eventually, the small house was expanded, and we gently brought our children into our little world, along with family and close friends. Our commitment to each other as this house grew didn't waver.

I discovered that my strengths became my weakness and my weakness became my strength. My independent streak needed to soften, because there was no way to get through Mark's illness alone. By allowing others to see me at my saddest and most vulnerable, I felt connected to others, particularly my children. By removing the barrier I built around myself, I grew.

DREAM: I am living in a five-hundred-year-old city. All the rooms in the city are small and rickety. In place of roads, there are gushing and rushing rivers. I am traveling alone in a small rickety boat. I am by myself.

CHAPTER THREE

Four Shadows

I HAVE ALWAYS HAD vivid premonitions about the future and people. The four premonitions below have stayed with me. At the time these events occurred, I didn't know a day would come when I would connect the dots and see them as touch points in my life. I refer to these events as the "Four Shadows." They indeed foreshadowed my later life.

In mystical Judaism, there is no before and no after. For instance, the Torah is understood as being given to Moses in one single moment, from the creation story to Moses's own death, before his death occurred. There is no backward or forward, according to Jewish mystics. Life is one moment that embraces the past as well as the future. In every moment is all of creation. In thinking about my experiences at ages thirteen, seventeen, twenty, and forty, it is as if my future visited me and prepared me for what was to come. Everything in life was, is, and will be. You have to embrace it all.

THIRTEEN YEARS OLD

A friend and I decided to volunteer at the Braille Institute of America, Inc., in Los Angeles. There were no training courses. We were asked to start the following week. I was assigned to help in the sewing room. I didn't have much sewing experience other than a home economics class in seventh grade. I walked in and decided to help an elderly woman I saw sitting alone across the room.

I remember walking across the linoleum floor toward her. She was sitting apart from the other adults at a table by herself. She told me she had recently lost her sight. Her scowl and tone of voice clearly expressed anger and bitterness about her blindness. She was also angry that she was placed in a class to learn to sew.

The class project was hand-sewing a clown from little round pieces of cloth. The thread was stitched around the circular edge and then pulled toward the center. The cloth disc had a tiny hole in the middle so it could be threaded down a string of yarn to complete arms and legs. A plastic clown head was attached at the top.

"Why teach a blind person to sew?" she asked me. "We're going to prick ourselves and not even see what we've made."

I had to wing it with a sensible answer. I sat very close to her and asked if she had a grandchild.

"Yes, I have a granddaughter," she said.

"Why not make the clown for her? She'll see the clown and love it. I'll help you. We'll do it together."

I volunteered once a week for a semester. Each week, the woman and I sat side by side, talking and sewing. Over time, her attitude softened, and we shared laughs. By the end of the semester, she finished the clown doll, and her granddaughter loved it.

During the months I sat with her, I didn't want her to be bitter and angry. Working with her brought out an innate gentleness and patience I didn't know I had. I felt a connection to her by sitting beside her, making her laugh while we created something together.

Like Mark, she was given a disability late in life. My work with her showed me I had the skills I needed to help support Mark as he declined.

SEVENTEEN YEARS OLD

During my last year of high school, I volunteered at Rancho Los Amigos Hospital in Downey, California. It was a hospital for physically disabled people. Each Sunday, I drove the forty-five-minute commute to help on the children's ward. The children who lived there ranged from five to eighteen years old. They were severely disabled,

I was considering becoming a special education teacher and already had four years of volunteer experience with special-needs children. I felt more connected and comfortable with people with disabilities than with my teenaged peers. At Rancho Los Amigos, I helped feed the children, played games, and created art projects. Those were some of my happiest hours at that time in my life.

An all-out favorite activity of the children was a game of volleyball I devised with a small net and balloons. I'd place a group of the children on one side of the net, all of them in wheelchairs or lying on gurneys. I was on the other side of the net, tossing the balloons back and forth with the children.

As each balloon was tossed my way, I'd exaggerate diving on the floor or falling backward in my attempt at tossing the balloon back to them. Each slip and slide of mine created howls of laughter on their side. I'd laugh too. They didn't want the game to end. It was fun for all of us!

During this time, I developed a friendship with a seventeen-year-old boy named Mark. He was exactly my age, yet our lives were worlds apart. He'd had his left leg amputated, and his ability to speak was extremely limited. Even so, we related well with each other and spent hours together each Sunday.

There was an envelope in the side drawer of his bedside table. It was a letter from his mother. Each Sunday, he'd point to the drawer and, with muffled, slurred speech, tell me he received a new letter from his mother and asked if I would read it to him. I knew it was the same letter I had read to him many times before. Perhaps he did too. I never knew. Each time, I'd act surprised and excited and happily read the "new" letter to him. His smile would bloom. After I read the letter, I'd place him in his wheelchair and push him up and down the corridors of the hospital. He'd yell, "Faster," and I'd run faster. I'd make sharp turns, and he'd squeal with laughter.

My last day of volunteering was sudden. I arrived on Sunday and visited with Mark. His other leg had been amputated during the week between our visits. I was stunned. I finished my day, returned to my car, and cried all the way home. I never returned to Rancho Los Amigos again. I never said goodbye to him. I regret I didn't thank him for what he taught me.

The young Mark allowed me to bring joy into his life. I was totally at ease being with someone who had a disability. Because of what I learned being with this courageous young man, I was able to give the best of myself to my husband throughout his illness.

TWENTY YEARS OLD

When I was twenty years old, my parents, older sister Caren, and I were on a cruise. Each family was seated at the same table each night for dinner. We were seated near another family. I looked up and saw four children, a wife, and a husband. The father was sitting in a wheelchair.

Instantly, my body chilled to the bone. I was transfixed, motionless, and I felt caught off guard. The father was wearing a pale gray suit. I can still see his soft gray hair. I've seen plenty of people in wheelchairs and disabled people, but this chill went through me differently. It was a jolt to my body, a kind of knowing, a tap or shake-up in my soul.

I never forgot this man or his family. I silently watched them each night for two weeks. Now, I can't help but wonder, was it a preview of my future and somehow I knew it?

Thirty-five years later, Mark and I were on a cruise ship, crossing the Atlantic Ocean together on the *Queen Mary*. He used a wheelchair and scooter to make his way around the ship. We dined in the dining room and had our regular table. It was the premonition: my life as I had seen it thirty-five years earlier.

I now wonder if Mark and I were a foreshadowing for someone else's life.

FORTY YEARS OLD

Mark and I moved to Raleigh, North Carolina, from Los Angeles, and we were standing in the foyer of the temple we had joined a few days earlier. We didn't know a single person. A large group had gathered near us. I heard a voice rise above all the other voices, so I turned to listen and saw a man place an arm around another man, and I overheard him say: "I'm a neurologist, the kind of doctor you hope never to see. You don't want to have to make an appointment with me."

When I overheard that doctor speak, I felt a panic. I didn't want to hear what the doctor said. Yet his words became tied to me, and I haven't been able to forget them.

Mark visited the same neurologist eight years later when the first symptoms of MSA appeared.

PART

II

MIDDLE STAGE:
DIAGNOSIS AND COPING

CHAPTER FOUR

September 28, 2011

OUR THIRD VISIT TO Mayo Clinic in September 2011 was pivotal. As we prepared to go, we knew the final diagnosis would be given, and we were pretty certain what the diagnosis would be. The day before leaving, we were at the kitchen table, talking and crying, when the doorbell rang. It was our daughter, Emily. When we saw Emily standing there, we knew there was only one way to be, and that was to be ourselves and to be honest about what was happening and how we were feeling.

"You can be real with Emily. It's okay," I said.

I don't think she'd ever seen Mark this upset.

To add to the unease we were already feeling, we were informed that we would be meeting with a new doctor. Dr. Low was moving into full-time research and transferring his patients' care to his colleague, Dr. Paola Sandroni, whom we had never met.

I was always included in each visit with Mark, but this time, the nurse asked me to stay in the waiting room. I watched her accompany Mark, who was by now using two walking sticks to maintain his balance, toward

Dr. Sandroni's office. I couldn't take my eyes off the long hallway into which Mark disappeared. Mark was alone with the new doctor, while I was outside in the waiting room. I felt anxious waiting for the nurse to come back and take me to meet with Dr. Sandroni and Mark. I wanted to know what was happening.

Eventually, the nurse came and asked me to follow her. The door to the exam room opened. Mark was sitting on a bench, leaning against the wall as though he had fainted or had been punched. I knew he had been given the diagnosis: he looked pale and in shock. I sat next to him and held his hand. He moved his head slowly in my direction and said, "I have MSA. This is surreal."

I cried.

We both looked at Dr. Sandroni.

She said she had something else important to tell us. There was a double-blind clinical trial occurring through Mayo Clinic, and Dr. Low was at the helm. It was for the drug rifampicin. There was hope it might slow the progression of MSA. She wanted to know whether Mark would like to participate in this study.

She had handed us a glimmer of hope. We were so dazed we could hardly respond, but we made an appointment with Dr. Low for the next day to learn more about the study. We left Dr. Sandroni's office in shock. We walked hand in hand toward his next appointment. Mark was scheduled for an MRI.

While walking to the radiology area, I got a text from our friend Roxanne. She and her husband, Dan, had driven from St. Paul, where they live, to join us for dinner in Rochester and offer support. They were heading to our favorite Italian restaurant in Rochester, Victoria's, to meet us for dinner.

When I got their text, I wasn't sure what to do. Should I leave Mark while he was having his MRI? He read my thoughts and said the MRI would take at least an hour. It might be good for me to be with them rather than alone.

I dropped Mark off at his appointment and called Roxanne. I poured out syllables, not words. I was babbling. I was aware I wasn't lucid. I said I would meet them in a few minutes. Roxanne told me later my voice was strange sounding, heavy, intense, and low-pitched: a voice you might hear in a horror movie. My voice was not in my body.

I managed to find my way to the restaurant. Roxanne and Dan were standing out in front. I collapsed into their arms and sobbed. We didn't go into the restaurant. I don't remember what they said, just that they held me for a long time. Eventually, we decided to find Mark. We arrived in the waiting room of the clinic just as Mark was finishing. I found an unused exam room down the hall, and the four of us went inside the darkened room. We all cried. Mark asked to be alone with me. He told Roxanne and Dan we would meet them at Victoria's in forty-five minutes.

Once alone, Mark and I held each other and cried. Mark said he couldn't believe he would be facing such a horrible disease. He knew he would end up completely incapacitated, unable to walk, talk, swallow, or move his limbs.

When he stopped crying, he heartbreakingly asked, "In the future, will you clean my face?"

I tearfully answered, "Yes."

But Mark's trajectory was also unpredictable. The path through MSA is different for every person. There are plateaus, valleys, and avalanches when a new symptom appears.

Joining Roxanne and Dan at Victoria's, we ordered our favorite drink: brandy Alexanders. It's usually an after-dinner drink, but on that day, we wanted them right away. His health gone, Mark joked and ordered what we came to call "what the fuck" pizza with everything on it. That evening with our friends was intimate and warm. We even had some laughs. After dinner, Roxanne and Dan drove back to their home in St. Paul.

The next day, I wandered the halls alone at Mayo Clinic while Mark had another test. I felt lost. I stepped into a meditation room and tried walking the labyrinth outlined on the floor. I lay flat in the center of the labyrinth and stared at the whirling colors on the ceiling. My chest felt tight. I tried breathing slowly. I reminded myself that I just have this moment. I didn't know about the future. I allowed myself to feel vulnerable and not let fear take over. I was very good at taking care of others; I'd need to learn to take care of myself.

I left, walked down a few more hallways, and stumbled into the chaplain's office.

"Can I help you?" asked a woman sitting at a desk.

I turned toward the voice and burst into tears. I nodded.

She took me into a dimly lit room. A woman dressed in regular clothes came into the room and sat across from me. She asked if I believed in the afterlife.

"Whoa, not so fast," I answered.

I asked her for guidance for the here and now. I needed to know how to navigate my life with a husband with a terminal illness, and how to talk to my children and Mark. When would be the best time to break the news to our children, and what words to use? Jeremy was twenty-seven and had gotten engaged to Jenn. Emily was twenty-five; she and James had returned to North Carolina from DC and were living in Durham. David was twenty and had transferred from University of Pittsburgh to UNC–Chapel Hill starting his junior year.

I wanted to know how to live with worry and sadness and face my future. We spoke for about an hour. I needed to meet Mark. The chaplain walked with me through the building to where Mark was waiting for me. The three of us were going to meet the next day.

We had told the children we would call them that evening to tell them about the final diagnosis. Mark told them in a straightforward way that he had been diagnosed with MSA. He was quick to assure them it was not genetic, but he also took the time to explain what it was.

"Now I know what I'm going to die from," he added.

I spoke too. We took turns, depending on which one of us was not crying. It was the hardest phone call we had ever made together. I closed the curtains in our hotel room and hid under the covers. I was quiet. I didn't want to talk to anyone. Mark, on the other hand, needed to talk. Once the kids knew, he felt it was time to call our other family members and close friends. While I hid, he systematically made one phone call after another.

After Mark made all the calls, I asked him whether he was depressed. He said no. I told him I wasn't either. We had the same reaction. We were sad and in shock but not depressed. The phone calls were cathartic for him. Around midnight, I ordered room service.

Since Mark was going to be in the double-blind research study, we had to extend our stay until the following Tuesday. Mark had more tests to undergo, and the medication for the study had to arrive from Tennessee. The waiting games were about to begin.

The next day, the chaplain I had met had to cancel at the last minute. We were desperate, so I called the chaplain's office and asked who was on call.

"Father Byrne" was the response.

"I'll take him!" I said.

During the next three days, while we waited for tests and drugs, we met with three chaplains of three different faiths: a Catholic priest, a Lutheran minister, and a Jewish rabbi. They all shared an understanding of the cycle of life—how it is filled with happiness and touched by sorrow and struggles. We talked about how life is complex; there is light and darkness, fear and insight, aloneness and togetherness. We talked about how we cannot be shielded, nor can we shield others from illness, life, and death. We talked about how, in order to evolve and gain insight and compassion, we must experience it all. Everybody is going to die. Some just have more information beforehand.

Of all of them, Father Byrne had the best insights about our children. He counseled us that, if they were like us, they would remain strong, compassionate, and loving toward us. He told us he believed they would handle this struggle with strength, insight, and love, just as we were doing. He said he knew they would be fine; they would be sad because they would have learned from us how to love deeply.

He was right.

After spending two hours with Father Byrne, I was on a spiritual high.

We had arrived at Mayo Clinic the day before Rosh Hashanah and returned home a few evenings before Yom Kippur. The days between these Holy Days are considered the most introspective and personally reflective time of the year. They are called the "Days of Awe." There we were, at Mayo Clinic facing the worst diagnosis in the world: a drawn-out and fatal illness. We were contemplating Mark's end of life. I wondered if this kind of confrontation of life and death is what was really at the root of the Jewish idea of the Days of Awe.

Part of being in the research study meant returning to Mayo Clinic twice over the next year. Mark would have monthly blood tests at home taken at a local lab and biweekly phone conversations about his changing health with Dr. Low.

We were feeling a bit of hope and relief. Perhaps Mark would be part of a study that cures MSA. Perhaps this new medication would slow the progression of this horrible disease. Perhaps we were lucky to be at the right place at the right time. Wrong! (Like many drug trials, this one didn't provide a cure. But we didn't know this yet).

Since Mark got into the clinical trial, we needed to stay longer than originally planned. I let Roxanne know, and she invited us to St. Paul for the weekend. She said we could stay with them and see her perform in the play *Church Basement Ladies.*

We rented a car and made the drive. We needed an escape.

On Saturday night, the four of us drove to the Plymouth Playhouse; Mark and I sat next to Dan in the back row of the 250-seat theater. At one point, the rubber cake prop Roxanne was supposed to cut accidentally bounced off the table. The audience burst into laughter. The laughter shook me a little because it felt surreal but oddly welcome in our long days of sadness.

The day before our return home, I asked for as many purple "Cure MSA" rubber wristbands as the nurses could give me. I wanted to bring dozens home and hand them out to everyone we knew. The nurse gave me four. I showed them to Mark.

"They only had four? This must be a rare disease," he quipped.

All five kids planned on being at our house when we arrived home Tuesday night. I spoke with Emily a few days before our return.

"We won't be sitting shiva[5] Tuesday night," I said. "Dad and I want to hear all about Jeremy and Jenn's wedding plans, as well as all the other things that have been going on while we have been away."

When we pulled into the driveway, all five of them ran to greet us with smiles, tears, and open arms. As we sat around the dining table, Mark spoke

---

5 Shiva is the traditional Jewish period of mourning when family and friends gather in the home to remember the deceased and surround the family with love, prayers, and support.

of starting a new career. I was thinking, he's fifty-five years old with a fatal illness and he's talking about starting a new career? His goal, he said, was to find purpose in this situation and not wither away. He said he wanted to write a book on patient advocacy from the patient's perspective.

He continued to tell the kids that having MSA would not define him or our family. He reminded them to live their lives according to their own desires, not his disease. Mark insisted David follow through with his plans to travel in Europe and study in Spain. He told Jeremy, Emily, James, and Jenn each to live their lives as they chose. He declared his disease should not derail their plans.

"I've beat one fatal illness," he added, referring to his tonsil cancer. "I can beat another."

After he spoke, the kids sat close to Mark. I moved away to let them be near him.

Mark asked only one thing of all of us: do not Google MSA. He said he was afraid the information on the internet could be wrong or distorted. Looking back, I realize there was more to Mark's request. He simply wanted to shield them from the ghastly particulars of this awful disease.

Barely Moving

I'm stuck inside a ball
in the air
looking at the underside
of falling leaves

I blow hard
finally
I move an inch
I blow again
and again

Drizzle to downpour
Clouds of illness
Blocking sunlight

CHAPTER FIVE

Mantra

EVEN WITH MARK'S GOOD cheer, we were both living a nightmare. He looked worried, even in his sleep. One night as I was going to bed, my heart was racing, I couldn't take a breath, I felt dizzy and anxious. It felt like a heart attack. After speaking with a doctor, I learned I had had my first panic attack. I started taking Xanax as needed and Ambien at night. As Mark's health deteriorated, I was trying to find my footing. All my usual anchors were gone. I felt untethered. There were no "shoulds" and no "coulds" anymore; there were just days to live through. As my life shattered, I had to find the glue.

Mark and I were fifty-five and no longer making plans for an empty nest or a fun retirement together. MSA had pushed our dreams aside and left us wandering in a wilderness of what was to come and how we would love each other through it. At each wicked turn of the disease, we found we had to stop, regroup, and try to figure out what to do, while being gentle with ourselves and with each other. We were healthy and excited by life and living until we were bitch-slapped by MSA.

As the days turned into months and then years, I learned a hard lesson: the future will take care of itself. Our goal is to take care of the present. MSA handed me two jobs. One, taking care of Mark. The other, finding my new separate self. For the first time I could remember, fear was entering my life. I could not hide or run from it. I had trouble going places where there might be a large group, which was not like me at all. I usually became energized by groups of people. I noticed my breathing would change when I was in a large group. I developed a mantra to say at times when I felt like I was dissolving: strength, stamina, wisdom, and acceptance. Later, I added "humor" to my list of words. To prepare myself for each new day, as soon as I woke up, I started saying the same mantra: strength, stamina, wisdom, acceptance, and humor.

For many years, my totem had been the butterfly. The butterfly represents personal transformation and the ability to go through changes with grace, lightness, and playfulness. I added another totem. (Who says you can't have two?) I needed a totem with legs, one that can stand on its own two feet. Something solid. Perhaps a deer. The deer has the ability to be vigilant, move quickly, and trust its instincts to get out of the trickiest situations.

During this same time, Mark began meditating before falling asleep at night. He listened to music and created a mantra. I had created a mantra to help me cope, but I had never told Mark about it. It surprised me that he, too, had a mantra to soothe him at the end of his day.

I am here
I am healing
I am healthy
I am loved
I am loving
I am strong
I am surviving
I am I am I am

CHAPTER SIX

Friends and Therapy

ONE DAY, I WAS driving alone in Raleigh. My mind was filled with worries about Mark while tears poured down my face. I no longer remembered what errands I was supposed to do. I was driving aimlessly, not recognizing where I was or the direction I was heading. It began to rain. I noticed I liked the sound of the rain on the metal roof of my car. I made a left turn into the first parking lot I saw. It was the most sterile strip mall imaginable. I pulled into a random parking space right by the Dollar Store. The weather was cold, wet, and gray. I noticed a dark blue tattered beach towel lying on the passenger seat. I reclined my seat and covered myself with the towel. I closed my eyes and soothed myself by listening to the rain.

My book club was scheduled to meet two days after our return from Mayo Clinic. My book club has been meeting since 1996, and over the years, everyone had experienced and shared some personal tragedy. Although I was emotionally drained by what we had just learned regarding the diagnosis, I knew I needed to go to book club and share the news of Mark's illness that night. But I wasn't sure how to do so.

Before the meeting, I went to dinner with my friend Carla. During our meal, I told her about Mark's diagnosis and asked whether she would help me tell the group if I couldn't. She agreed. When it was time for things to start, I grabbed her arm, we hid in a nearby room, and I cried. I didn't think I could talk in public about Mark. She assured me she would speak for me if I needed her help.

Like always, we sat in a circle, taking turns to discuss the recent book we had read. As my turn drew near, my heart began to beat faster. My breathing became more rapid. I thought I was going to faint. My thoughts were bursting inside my head. I began questioning whether I should share Mark's diagnosis in front of a group.

When it was my turn to speak, my eyes darted around the room. I felt on fire. One woman said, "What is it, Julia?" I looked at Carla and gave her a nod indicating I needed her to help me speak. She started to explain my recent visit to Mayo Clinic.

I interrupted her. I realized that it was my story and I needed to be able to tell it. There were tears, but I got through the whole thing. I can remember everybody looking at me. When I stood up, everyone circled around me and hugged me. I felt relief that the secret I had been carrying for so many years had at last been given a name.

I met with my first therapist regularly for close to six months after our first visit to Mayo. Then, I took a break. Looking back, I realize that I probably stopped at this point because the therapist was pushing me uncomfortably close to important matters.

As Mark's health declined, I needed someone to talk with who was an expert on end-of-life issues: my second therapist, who, upon hearing about Mark's illness and my coping mechanisms, nodded occasionally.

"You're doing great. I give you an A-plus."

I met with him only once. I needed more than a report card.

The third therapist was a board-certified psychiatrist with a particular interest in grief and bereavement, as well as the role of spirituality in healing. After reading about her training and her philosophy on her website, I felt she might be able to help and guide me.

Her office was in the back of her home, on a tree-lined street in a historic neighborhood. I pulled to the front of the purple and yellow house—my favorite colors!—and walked along a stone path to her backyard garden. Her office was filled with books, plants, velvety furniture, colorful paintings, unusual trinkets, and hanging mobiles.

She greeted me warmly. I instantly thought she had the perfect face for her profession—a bright expression, warm smile, and twinkling eyes. She was about my age and seemed to be a person who had experienced all the seasons of life. I trusted her immediately and didn't hesitate in talking with her. She became an important part of my healing puzzle. I went through dozens of tissue boxes in her office. I felt obliged to replace them, and on occasion, I did.

She told me a story about a sculptor. He had sculpted a perfect sphere from stone. After the stone was finished, the artist broke it into bits and then reassembled it using bolts. Now, fractured, it was finished and complete. The beauty is not in perfection. It is in our struggles. Our brokenness is universal.

After six months of meeting with her, while driving to my appointment along the winding road, I realized this was going to be my last appointment. The thought occurred in an instant, and it felt right. I wonder now if once again I was ending the therapy too soon. Was I avoiding something significant? Was I on the cusp of discovery and afraid?

When I arrived and sat in the same cozy armchair I always sat in, I told her this would be my last visit. I asked her if there was a way she likes to end a therapeutic term. She said she wanted the hour to highlight and reflect on the time we shared. As the hour came to a close, she became teary and said she didn't often learn from a client as she had with me. I thanked her. We hugged before I got into my car. As I drove away from her office, I thought I was going to be fine on my own, at least for now.

CHAPTER SEVEN

Pathways

DURING SUMMER 2011, THREE months before the official diagnosis but long after we knew something terrible was wrong and coming our way, I left Raleigh for two weeks to paint in Saugatuck, Michigan, at an art school called Oxbow. Mark flew with me. We spent the day exploring the little town of Saugatuck and walking along Lake Michigan. At that time, I felt he was steady enough to be without me for two weeks; he still drove and was capable of caring for himself.

Since the phone service was terrible at the school, I was off the grid. I didn't miss using a computer or phone. I needed the time away. I immersed myself in painting, hiking, and getting to know my instructors and fellow art students. I brought seven blank canvases with me. I felt as open as those canvases, waiting for the Oxbow experience to paint its life on me.

I took regular morning and evening hikes along the trails around the secluded campus, sometimes alone, sometimes with a fellow student. When I walked amid the trees, streams, and birds, I thought about Mark and our changing relationship. I worried about my life without Mark and how our children would be without a father. Even though I was off the grid, I was not escaping my fears of being alone or Mark's disease.

Mark and me at Oxbow, 2011.

Painting at Oxbow, 2011.

Being so far away from the day-to-day reality of my crumbling life, I found courage to tell some of the other artists at Oxbow that my husband had a terminal illness. My art allowed me to have a new voice.

Secluded Moment

During an isolated walk through the woods near Oxbow, I discovered an amazing pattern of light on the hilly path in front of me. I snapped a photo. Back in my studio, with a palette knife in each hand, I madly painted, angry and crying. I worked without stopping, finishing the painting in one afternoon.

On the top third of the painting, the rounded blue hill represented the earth with its dense woods. The crazy shapes of light reminded me of lightning bolts. On the bottom, in the center, is my shadow as I held the camera and shot the dark path ahead of me.

I made the rough shadows with thick dabs of paint smeared on. I created the jagged and harsh sunlight by leaving the stark white canvas unpainted. The broken shapes of light and dark and the tangle of trees became projections of the messy feelings inside my head. I titled it *Secluded Moment.*

Trees, Light, and Air or
Mark and I, A Double Portrait

On an evening walk, I spotted two trees. One was sturdy and tall, reaching toward the sun and sky. The other had fallen and was leaning heavily on the sturdier tree. I circled the two trees while the wind blew and leaves rustled.

I snapped a few photos. Later, in my studio, I painted these two trees. I knew this painting represented Mark and me: two intertwined trees, one fallen, one holding up the other.

These trees reminded me that our roles in life are not set in stone. Either one of us can be the sturdy tree or the fallen tree, depending on the time of day.

I used pink to show the glow of light that appears at the end of a day, or the end of a life. I painted a third tree in the composition, a gray ghost set higher, that seems to fly off the top of the painting. I used swirls of blue and green to represent the wind spiraling around the trees, representing the dizzy feeling I had as I walked my way through the woods. I titled this painting *Trees, Light and Air.* I also gave it a secret name: *Mark and I, A Double Portrait.*

A few nights before heading home, I had a dream. The dream had a title and several words, like a poem: *Land Escape. Purple, yellow, green, blue. Then along came red.*

I went to Oxbow in August 2011. In September, we went to Mayo Clinic and got the diagnosis of MSA. By November, Mark had stopped working. He shut down his office, much against his will. Many years before, as a self-employed businessman, he had had the foresight to take out a disability insurance policy, and it was now time to draw upon those benefits. (More on that topic later.) He was now officially a retired person but not overjoyed by the situation or the prospect of the loss of his professional identity.

Right after Mark closed his office, I had a one-woman art show I called "pathways" with my Oxbow paintings at a local restaurant known for its good food and support of local artists. I dedicated the show to Mark.

By then, all our close friends knew. On the night of the opening, Mark was no longer able to walk without aid and was using a cane. His balance was becoming more difficult, and he tired easily. To preserve his energy, Mark spent the evening sitting at a table, letting people approach him.

A group of friends joined Mark and me for dinner afterward at the restaurant. Jeremy and David were there too. Mark got up to use the restroom. Instantly, Jeremy's and David's eyes shifted to Mark. They waited for him to find his balance and make his way to the men's room before turning back to chatting with our fellow diners. It was a subtle shift, and the first of many transitions to come to our family. Like me, our children were becoming caregivers.

CHAPTER EIGHT

Giving

FRIENDS AND FAMILY ARRIVED almost daily when we returned from Mayo Clinic. In one day, a cake, two pies, and two pounds of chocolate were delivered to our home. A friend called that night and asked how Mark was doing. He answered, "Clogging my arteries." Given the new stream of visitors, Mark joked, "I'm more popular dead than alive."

After the diagnosis and art show, Mark began falling. I was in the shower the first time I saw him fall. He walked by and smiled beautifully. Suddenly, he lost his balance and fell. He couldn't stop himself. He fell gracefully and didn't hurt himself. I stood frozen under the warm water, watching helplessly. It happened so quickly, yet it looked as if life had switched to slow motion.

Mark got up and walked away without speaking a word. I followed, and we hugged a long time.

Mark asked over dinner one night, "You know what phase of life we're in?"

"No," I answered.

"You get whatever *you* want phase," he replied.

The next day, Mark suggested we go out to dinner at our favorite restaurant. After we sat down, he put a small gift bag on the table and handed me a sheet of paper that had been folded over and over several times. He told me to unfold it one fold at a time and to read what was there out loud. There were eight folds. This is what it said:

> *I'm special!!*
> *There's no one else like me!!*
> *I've been putting up with a lot of crap lately!!*
> *I deserve a present!!*
> *And, a nice dinner at my favorite restaurant!!*
> *I am loved by a lot of people!!*
> *So there!!*

Inside the bag was a beautiful double-stranded necklace and a bracelet made from purple and lavender crystals. He was the one facing a terminal illness, yet his concern was about taking care of me.

That was the essence of Mark. Generosity. Mark's core was golden. Mark began lighting a candle by his chair late at night as he meditated. The candle created a glow. It was like Mark's golden soul.

CHAPTER NINE

Untethered

MARK WAS ESSENTIAL TO me. He and I were on our own treacherous paths, having our own treacherous nightmares. He was facing his death, and I was facing life alone as a widow. Sometimes I felt adrift and untethered. Other times, Mark kept me tethered and connected to him. Together, we were tethered to life.

I felt soft inside and out. Without a protective wall around me, I was cloudlike, absorbing all the sadness like droplets of rain. Mark had always been my earth and ground, light and certainty. He was strength and determination. He was clarity. He answered my questions. He held me up.

Some days, it was unbearable to watch Mark struggle. I was often left speechless. I needed a strong will during this heart-wrenching process but didn't know where to find it. One day, I was working on something on the computer and, out of nowhere, I smashed the keyboard, then threw the computer across the room. It didn't break. Sometimes my inner balance was so wobbly, I could feel dizzy while taking a bite of food. One day, while going up the sixteen steps to the second floor of our home, I ate an entire candy bar.

Storm

Something inside of me is breaking
Exploding pieces and
bits of ash surround me
My life is a storm
A fire
with spinning black clouds
I'm on an unknown journey
in the middle of nowhere
Twisted shadows are on the wall
blowing at my stomach
Sudden noises
splinter my swarming thoughts
Rotten smells churn my nightmares

DREAM: There is an unbelievably small, furry, and cute kitten in my bedroom on the carpet. Above, there is my painting with a tree on the right and a turtle on the left. To the left of the turtle is a 3-D color image of a brain. Real leaves from the tree are falling slowly off the painting. My son David helps me as more kittens appear. Six unbelievably cute and furry puppies appear, as well as dozens of short black worms. The worms are deathlike and scary.

DREAM: I'm driving home. As I approach my home, I see two huge furry dogs on the street in front of my house; they are almost the size of horses. I can tell they will eat me alive if I get near them. I find another way to enter my house.

The next scene in the dream: I'm in a narrow bed. I'm alone. Mark isn't next to me. My eyes are closed, but I can see through my eyelids. A pack of flesh-eating dogs run and pounce on me. I'm scared to death.

While keeping my eyes closed, I move my hand slowly to gently pat the dogs so they don't eat me alive. They are all across my body. I want to call out to Mark. I'm afraid.

DREAM: The word furious was spelled frivolous.

DREAM: I am in a two-story structure made of ice. Jeremy is helping me find three people from the second floor who could help me understand what to do about the difficult situation I am facing with Mark. The three people are late. I wonder where they are. I ask Jeremy to help me find them. I need answers to my questions. One woman arrives and looks directly into my eyes. At that moment, I hear a terrifyingly loud noise. I look up—a huge avalanche is falling rapidly toward me. Suddenly it freezes and stops midair, six feet or so above me.

DREAM: I'm sitting on a flat wooden swing. It is not attached to a tree or anything. The metal chain is tied in knots and messed up. The swing begins to move through the air and water, indoors and outdoors, like a roller coaster. All five kids appear, and we're in a boat together. The crashing waves overflow onto the boat. The waves rise high, up to our shoulders. I run out of the boat and find stairs and yell to the kids to hurry out of the boat and up the stairway.

CHAPTER TEN

Breathing

I FEARED LOSING MARK and being separated from him forever. I began trying to gain control by breathing in the positive and breathing out the negative. The positives were my wonderful family and friends reaching out to me every step of the way. They mailed me poems, left phone messages, invited me to the ballet, theater, lunches, and dinners. I went on walks through parks with friends. I poured my heart out many times to listening and caring ears. Some cried with me; others made me laugh and reminded me of my strength.

I breathed in acceptance and love, breathed out sadness and pain. This was my way of acknowledging the pain: to not fight against the despair I felt. It was the only way I could accept the course our life was on now.

Mark wanted to feel life. He wanted to experience it all until it was over. He said it was best for him to be in a good mood and have a good time in the present. He could no longer focus on the future. He tried hard to maintain that perspective. I also believe he was in a tremendous amount of pain knowing there was no future. To push through his own grief, he had to numb those difficult feelings. For Mark, numbness was like a shield.

This was in contrast to his life before his illness. As a small business owner, Mark had to keep an eye on the future. He would have failed if his focus had been only on the present.

I needed to balance being in the present and focusing on the future. Instead of my life becoming smaller as the details of Mark's care become greater, I had a strange sense my world was growing larger. I felt a peaceful strength growing within myself. I was preparing for a solo life and needed to carefully construct a solid foundation under my feet.

Mark and I had made a happy home together. I wanted this joy to continue. I was determined we would make each other feel safe. We would be kind. We would laugh. I believed this would balance our life and give meaning, peace, and preciousness to our remaining days together.

One day, while sitting with Mark and eating an orange, I looked up and saw him smiling. He said he was enjoying just looking at me. I wanted Mark and me to lift each other up and remain a light for the other. I wanted to feel we were in each other's loving hands. I was aware of the tangible moments with Mark: looking into each other's eyes, listening to each other, and embracing each other in the morning. Mark's presence was a comfort, even when he was down the hall or upstairs. There was an invisible band binding us to one another, no matter the physical distance.

CHAPTER ELEVEN

Traveling

This is so random. I feel like the wrong person to get this disease. Hey,
God, it's the other Mark Fr-i-efeld, not Mark Fr-e-ifeld.
My last name is always misspelled.

—MARK FREIFELD, 2011

IN MAY 2012, WE had plans to visit David during his junior semester
abroad in Spain and afterward take a cruise from London to New York
on the *Queen Mary*. As the trip got closer, Mark didn't want to leave
home. Whenever we talked about the trip, he pushed back and said he
thought we shouldn't go. I really wanted to go. After a tender discussion
one night about the trip, Mark finally acknowledged his true feelings.
He said he was mourning the loss of himself. We both cried.

When he shared these feelings with me, I told him his essence was
still there. His love of life, love of me, and love for our children, as well
as his humor and wit, were still present. It's all there, I told him. Please
continue to use your power, drive, and strength that have always been
the fire inside you. He said he felt like he was losing power.

The next day, I told Mark, "You are the dearest, most precious man.
Physically, you are less strong. There are physically abled people sleepwalk-
ing through life, like ghosts who have no passion, purpose, or intention.

MSA is a mental battle as much as it is a physical one; don't let the disease win the mental battle."

I reminded him that at Jeremy and Jenn's wedding the week before, Mark was his old self, even though he walked down the aisle with a cane and had to use a wheelchair for the first time to navigate around the hotel.

I told Mark, "Wake up each day as if it's Jeremy and Jenn's wedding day. Each day is a prize to be celebrated at the level of a son or daughter's wedding! As long as you're with me, we're going places, *living* our lives with friends, family, parties! We're going to make hay while the sun shines. Don't go down; bring your energy. *Do MSA differently.*"

We were in our bedroom talking the night before we left for Spain. Mark looked nervous. I moved closer to him, looked him in the eye, and said with confidence and comfort, "You're going, you're going, that's it, you're going. Get packed, you're going."

He didn't answer. He trusted me.

The idea for the trip to Spain and cruise on the *Queen Mary* was part of my new escapism philosophy, the beginning of my push to escape what had been handed to us. We needed new vistas and lively experiences outside the four walls of our home.

We had a glorious week in Madrid and Barcelona with David. David had a sixth sense about Mark and could anticipate his father's needs. He checked us in at the hotels, pushed Mark in the wheelchair, or allowed Mark to lean on him if they walked.

After a busy day of sightseeing, we returned to our hotel room in Barcelona. Mark became emotional, and David responded lovingly by placing his arm around him. I pulled back and sat quietly on the bed. Though no words were spoken, Mark was calmed and consoled by David. After a few moments, David and Mark turned to me and asked about our evening plans. They were prepared to stay in the hotel room. I said to both, "I've got our tickets. We're going to the flamenco performance!"

Looking back on my determination to take this trip and have fun, I can't believe how strong I was, all the while swimming through a terrible push-pull of anxiety that it was too much, too ambitious, just too hard for both of us.

After our week of traveling, David took us to the airport and said goodbye. We had to fly to England to board the *Queen Mary* on our own. Without David's help, I felt vulnerable. However, the wheelchair we had requested was at the airport in Barcelona when we arrived and when we landed in London. Mark was wheeled to the bus, which transported us to Southampton, the seaside town where the *Queen Mary* was moored. A wheelchair was waiting for us in Southampton to take us directly onto the ship. Seeing Mark in a wheelchair brought me back to my twenty-year-old self, seeing the woman push her husband up to the dinner table on the cruise, and realizing I was now that woman.

We arrived onboard and looked for the scooter we had ordered for Mark. It was not there. We were told to use a push wheelchair, which would have limited our freedom aboard ship. After I had several emotional and intense discussions with different people at the front desk, a scooter was located in a locked closet. Mark had never used a scooter before. It was new for Mark to be on his own without someone at his side to assist him. The scooter meant each of us could have a new sense of freedom.

On that first day, we did not communicate well about exactly when we'd meet up after our day of individual activities. I felt a panic arise and tears flow when Mark didn't appear in the room at a particular time. I became a total wreck. The porter had to console me. He made several phone calls to staff members, listing Mark as a missing person. Naturally, Mark showed up, and we discussed a way to leave notes for each other and keep in touch on board.

The *Queen Mary* gave me a new sense of myself. I had been eyeing the running track outside on Deck 7 during the first couple of days on the cruise. I'm not a runner; I don't even walk fast. I didn't know I had it in me to run. Yet there I was, running for more than an hour!

The wind blew strong and heavy against me. The ocean waves were high. The clouds were gray and full of rain. There was a drizzle on the path. The ship rocked in a way that made my legs heavy, but I pushed through and ran! To my surprise, it was delightful! My arms swung, my hair blew crazy in every direction, and my scarf swirled around my face. I maintained my balance and ran, my legs rocking with the rhythm of the ship. The wind pushed against my lower back like a heavy hand helping me run even faster. At one point I almost felt myself lifted by the wind's force and briefly thought I was going to fly. It scared me. I couldn't afford to blow away. Mark needed me, and I needed to be with him.

The last morning of the transatlantic crossing was spectacular. The ship arrived in New York just before dawn. Everyone on board planned where they wanted to stand to see New York's breathtaking skyline. I decided to be at the bow on Deck 11. I told Mark about where I wanted to stand. He said he didn't think he would be able join me because I always helped him get ready for the day, and it would take a long time. He hadn't gotten ready by himself for months.

I awoke at five, got dressed, and found my way to the deck alone. I had made the decision to do the things I wanted to do, even if I had to do them without Mark. I was trying to get used to experiencing things solo. I understood and accepted the reality that getting Mark ready for such an early morning event would be nearly impossible.

When I arrived at Deck 11, it was still pitch-black outside. Only a few people were there. I snapped photos with my cell phone to show Mark later.

Seeing the Statue of Liberty in the early morning light was a pivotal moment. I felt Mark's absence and realized I didn't want to have that moment without him. I pulled away from my front-row viewing spot and strolled the deck alone. The crowd was facing the Statue of Liberty, cheering. As I turned a corner, Mark was just opening a door to join me on the outside deck. The sun was starting to appear. We looked at each other and burst into tears. He's here; he made it somehow! He got himself dressed and on the scooter and used the two walking sticks up the elevator to Deck 11. We kissed and had our picture taken.

Mark and me on the *Queen Mary*, 2012.

When the ship pulled into New York, we caught a taxi to La Guardia Airport. After getting out of the taxi, I assisted Mark into a prearranged wheelchair while the cab driver unloaded our luggage and pulled away. Once I had Mark settled, I took a quick glance at our luggage. The most important piece was missing: the bag with Mark's lifesaving medicines.

I looked for the taxi driver. He had already driven off. I ran into the traffic, screaming for the taxi driver to stop. I cried to the luggage handlers at curbside. I pushed Mark to the gate and left him there. I ran down to the taxi manager's station. I was awash in tears as I explained about the luggage with all of my husband's medicines. I wondered why our driver hadn't returned to us immediately. The small piece of luggage was next to him in the passenger seat; I just knew he couldn't have missed it.

I ran back into the street, stopping every Indian taxi driver wearing a button-down shirt. Most of the taxi drivers were Indian with button-down shirts! In desperation, I blurted out to one driver, "What would make someone do a good deed?"

I ran back and forth between the taxi stand and our gate, checking on Mark and updating him on what was happening. I went through security so many times, I gave up and carried my shoes as I ran! Mark had been wheeled onto the plane and off again because I wasn't there to accompany him.

As emotional as I was, Mark was the complete opposite. He was quiet and calm. We missed our flight and were staring at my cell phone hoping the driver would call. My number was on the luggage tag. Suddenly my cell phone rang. It was the taxi driver returning with our suitcase. When he met me at the security gate, I hugged him with all my strength.

Fortunately, I didn't realize before our trip all the risks we'd face traveling with MSA. I only knew that if we'd stayed home, our routine would not have changed, and our lives would have stayed safe and the same. By the end of the cruise, Mark said he was getting to know himself better. We were both growing in the riptide of his illness.

CHAPTER TWELVE

"I'm good from the eyes up."

AFTER RETURNING FROM SPAIN, Mark realized he could no longer drive safely and, without telling me, sold his car. I came home one afternoon, and the car was gone. When I said something about the car, he responded lightheartedly, "Tell the earth to stop being so wobbly."

Shortly after the car was sold, we hired a young man to drive Mark to appointments—the ones where he didn't necessarily need me, such as the follow-up or minor test appointments and picking up medications at the pharmacy. By then, I had come to the realization that if I tried to do everything, I would be emotionally and physically wiped out.

One day, Mark and I decided we'd drive to our favorite burger joint in Durham. Mark was in the passenger seat, and I placed his travel wheel-chair in the trunk. When we arrived, I pulled the wheelchair out and rolled it near the passenger side. Once I got Mark safely in his seat, I happened to notice something on the floor of the passenger seat and turned away from him.

While I was searching for the item, the wheelchair, with Mark in it, began rolling down the slope toward the restaurant! As I turned back, I saw Mark was halfway down the incline! Mark, believing I was pushing him, had a tranquil expression on his face. Frantic, I raced to Mark and grabbed the handlebars of the wheelchair and began laughing crazily and hugging Mark. That was the day I learned there are brakes on the rear wheels.

As the illness sped up, our lives slowed down, and we learned to savor every minute we had together. Late one summer afternoon, we were sitting outside on our deck, under a clear blue sky and twinkling green leaves. The clouds floated above us. We talked about everything: our love, our loss, our missing each other, our strength, and our weaknesses. We held hands and our eyes met. He felt guilty for the pain he was causing and thought it was better to be a family doing fun things, creating happy memories, than thinking about death. I said, "Even though we just got back from our trip, you don't need to be in a special place to take an inspirational journey. That kind of journey can happen in our home with our family, friends, you and me. All I need to see is your smile. Absorb the love around you."

Close friends of ours, Orna and Randy, gave us the best gift: a family day joining them at their lake house at Lake Gaston. The morning we were scheduled to go, I was busy getting packed, loading the car, filling ice chests, organizing food, medicines, maps, iPhones, clothing, as well as cleaning this and that around the house and car. It took me almost three hours. Mark was sitting on a barstool in the kitchen silently watching me. I began getting tense and slammed a couple of cabinet doors and drawers.

"Getting uptight, Nurse Ratched?" Mark asked. All the tension went away, and he made me laugh at myself. I was in awe of Mark's beautiful spirit.

The children drove together from Durham, where they all lived, while Mark and I drove from our house. As we neared the cabin, we saw signs on the side of the road welcoming us to "Camp Freifeld."

Once we arrived, Mark needed help getting out of the car and into the house. After we got him settled, the kids and I unloaded everything. Mark and I enjoyed a day of laughs as we rode on our friends' boat and watched the kids jet skiing, tubing, and waterskiing. The weather was gorgeous, the food was delicious, and to top it off, we took a picture of each of us wearing one of Mark's special raunchy T-shirts.

Mark had a rather quirky T-shirt collection that started randomly when a T-shirt in a store window caught his eye while we were visiting Jeremy in New York City. (At the time, Jeremy was twenty-three and pursuing a career in music.) Mark thought the shirt was just the perfect expression of frustration for one of those special moments in life: "Fuck You You Fuckin' Fuck."

The shirt made him throw his head back in laughter, but he didn't buy it. A few months later, Jeremy sent Mark the shirt for Father's Day. The other kids started finding and sending him T-shirts with the word "fuck" somewhere on them. One of his nieces sent a shirt. Several friends sent shirts. I also added to Mark's collection. The shirts came from travels around the world. We all found it funny because Mark was rarely one to swear in real life. But Mark loved this collection of T-shirts; in fact, the whole family loves them.

From left to right: Emily, James, Jenn, Jeremy, me, Mark, and David.

CHAPTER THIRTEEN

The Mikvah

I CONTINUED MY JOURNEY through Mark's illness by adding the mikvah immersion ritual to my life. A mikvah, also known as "gathering of waters," is an ancient Jewish tradition of taking a ritual bath marking times of joy, as well as sadness. This ritual can be used to mark a time of change and personal transformation. Rather than going for a one-time experience, I signed up for the one-year take-all-the-mikvahs-you-want membership. My hope was that I would discover an inner strength and resiliency to deal with Mark's illness and how our lives were unfolding at home. I felt adrift and needed to gather and soften the fraying and torn edges of myself. With the help of the mikvah ritual, I was open and ready to welcome my true feelings.

I imagined that the beauty of the ritual, done in the prescribed ways and times, would create a new calm and rhythm in my life. My life felt horrible: jarring and discordant. Through the mikvah, I was seeking rhythms of continuity and peace.

I decided to go to the mikvah every other Tuesday evening. On my drive to the mikvah, the stars would appear, and everything felt calmer. I wanted the experience to begin on my drive there and continue until I came home and crawled under the bedcovers.

The mikvah guides were all soft-spoken women. They welcomed me each time with a hug and caring conversation. I began to schedule my appointments to coincide with one guide named Susan. I had crossed paths with her years earlier, and she felt comfortable, familiar, and lovely to me. Her gaze was steady. We shared laughs, tears, and prayers. She informed me that, prior to my arrival, she recites the Shehecheyanu, a prayer of gratitude. The mikvah is a holy place, and she felt she needed to prepare herself and the place for the moment the guest arrives.

My appointment always began with an intimate heart-to-heart with Susan in the waiting room. This room was dimly lit and cozy. Part of the mikvah ritual is selecting a prayer to say during the immersion. Some people bring their own prayers. Each time, I would select two laminated prayer cards from the box provided. There was an array of prayer cards for various life transitions: becoming a bride/groom/parent/grandparent, or going through divorce, conversion, and so on. I chose ones on healing and gratitude.

I entered the preparation room alone. This room was also softly lit and welcoming. There was a colorfully painted table on which to place personal items. There were shelves stocked with every bath item imaginable: towels, sheets, toothpaste, soaps, shampoo, hair dryer, Q-tips, combs, and mouthwash.

There was a framed sheet of the seven preparatory meditations on one of the shelves. While reading the seven meditations, I followed the guidelines and steps: wipe off makeup and nail polish, take off earrings and bracelets, and remove clothing and coverings. I bathed, rinsed, and scrubbed in the shower. There would be nothing between my body and the water. I looked at myself in the mirror and smiled. I said in Hebrew, *"Hineini,"* which means "Here I am."

I wrapped myself in a cream-colored sheet and stepped into the third room, the mikvah room. There was an open window high on the wall between the immersion room and the gathering room. In the gathering room, family or friends may sit silently and hear and be present for your mikvah.

The mikvah is traditionally made up of two wells: the collection well, where the rainwater is collected, and the immersion well. I removed the sheet and walked slowly down the seven steps into the immersion well. The water was warm; it reached my neck. I was suspended, buoyant, and embraced. I stared into the shadowy blue water. I read the prayers on the special prayer cards I had selected about the holiness of the body. In the mikvah, all bodies are holy; even diseased bodies are holy. There's a wholeness in the ritual.

The size of the mikvah is just right for one person. It's a solitary and interior experience. When I was there, I was alone and naked in an enclosed room immersed in water. I was silent and cocooned in my own thoughts, dreams, and wishes, listening to my own singular voice speak prayers aloud. The feeling in the mikvah was one of give and take with self and soul. I felt alone and wanted to pray alone.

By going to the mikvah, I knew I was preparing for a solo life. The prayer cards included messages for caregiving, illness, renewal, and new journeys. Being enveloped by water made me buoyant in both body and spirit.

One night, while in the mikvah and reading the prayer cards, I noticed something different about the words. I had accidentally taken cards about celebrating joyous transitions instead of the usual cards I took for healing and gratitude.

Surprisingly, the words rang true. They spoke of landing on your feet, a song in your heart, and being circled by loving family and friends. I was finding firm ground, the song inside me had not been extinguished, and I had loving people surrounding me.

The seemingly accidental selection of these cards reminded me of how truth is revealed and understood. Instead of joy being the opposite of sadness, perhaps joy and sadness are interconnected and interdependent. Perhaps joy cannot exist without sadness, or humor without despair.

I floated then moved gracefully below the surface. The mikvah water caught my tears. I read two more prayers and dipped below the surface twice as prescribed in the ritual. I emerged from the mikvah, dried myself off, and got dressed, adding the layers of my everyday life. Leaving the mikvah, I walked back into the night, stepping into the world again.

I was ready to part with the mikvah ritual as my one-year membership was coming to an end. The purpose of this ritual had been fulfilled. I was less unhinged, more connected to myself.

My heart felt heavy when I went for my last mikvah on the day before we began hospice care. I felt withdrawn and like a fluttering brittle leaf as I stood before my mikvah guide. Susan and I both knew it would be my last mikvah, and we were getting ready to part. I could tell my feelings weren't free-flowing. I felt tight, clutched. I glanced at her and said, "Thank you. I'll see you again." I couldn't say goodbye.

CHAPTER FOURTEEN

Gardening

FOR YEARS, MARK AND I took walks together in our neighborhood. After Mark got sick, I continued walks in our neighborhood solo. Initially, I stared at the street and barely noticed anyone passing by. Later, I started to look intently at gardens: flowers, trees, hedges, grasses, and shrubs. All the growing things.

Previously, I had not noticed the intricacies of plant life and the language of gardening: perennials, annuals, "new growth on old wood," double bloomers, and variegated leaves. Walk by walk, I began turning into a gardener.

I fantasized about gardens and nurseries while I was at home and when I was driving in the car. I found myself wanting to go to gardening stores just to look and learn, walking up and down the aisles. Later, I started buying plants. I would go alone, because having anyone else with me was distracting from the intense enjoyment I felt browsing the rows of flowers and plants.

I once met someone who added a piercing to her ear at every new stressful juncture in her life. My life was stressful, but instead of adding piercings, I began adding flowers and plants to my front yard. After a year, I had added more than a hundred plants!

There is a rhythm to religious rituals and a rhythm to planting a garden. Like the mikvah, the garden is a place where you can bring your imagination. You invent the necessary purpose for the garden and the plants you choose.

The mikvah nurtured my soul and interior life. The garden brought me back to the physical world. After I finished with the mikvah, planting a garden was the next step in my journey, and it was a give and take with the natural world. I began spending time outdoors, hearing birds and the rustling of leaves, and feeling breezes. I paid attention to the change of the seasons.

I taught myself about companionable gardens. Some plants stunted the growth of a nearby plant. More suitable plants complemented and strengthened their neighbors. Those types of gardens mature beautifully in form and color. Mark and I were like a companionable garden. The two of us, side by side, had blossomed together and brought out the best in each other. We were balanced and harmonious.

After all the planting during spring and fall, I knew there was a waiting period before I could see the results of my work. Gardens become dormant in the winter and renew and grow in spring. By the following spring, I was eager to see the new life: the little shoots of green and cheery tiny petals.

I had a new awareness that the nighttime is when magic happens in a garden. At night, the plants use the sun's stored energy; as night moves toward daylight, they can grow, expand, and unfurl their leaves and petals. Seedlings are not quietly sleeping at night. They may look inactive, but they are busy. It takes energy and power for a seedling to make its way upward to the surface, defying gravity, pushing through the dark dense earth, and seeking the sun.

I ran out of the house every morning to check on my budding plants, my little babies. The first clue of new growth showed itself in the way the pine straw would circle around the struggling seedling in the garden bed. Every morning, I would lift the whirls of pine straw and discover a baby green shoot. New life!

I often snapped photos of the ever-evolving beautiful blooms and greenery and texted them to Mark. There were gifts galore greeting me in the garden each morning.

CHAPTER FIFTEEN

Equal Parts Pain and Joy

MY LIFE WAS YIN and yang. In the darkness, there was a speck of light. In the light, there was a speck of darkness. It was never all one or the other. While we had not expected a fatal illness, I couldn't believe how my world was broadening and not narrowing. My journey was beginning, not ending. My life was taking fascinating and terrifying turns.

The yin and yang philosophy reminded me of breaking the glass at a Jewish wedding. In the exact moment of intense love and joy, there is a moment of shattered sadness to remember: the crumbling of the ancient Temple and the broken pieces of the world. At a Jewish funeral, we recite prayers praising life and all its beauty.

Mark and I came from secular homes and, as a couple, found meaning in Jewish living. We took classes and learned about holidays, culture, and other rituals to include in our daily life. We embraced Shabbat on Friday evenings, gathering our family and friends around our dining table.

Jewish rituals were anchors when I felt adrift. They offered me comfort and structure during moments of pain and sadness. The warmth and familiarity of communal rituals tapped into my senses. Reciting sacred words was calming and being surrounded by family and friends healed me. The mikvah was a private and solitary ritual. This experience allowed me to go inward, with easier access to my feelings. The rituals guided me, becoming touch points along my path of grief.

Another outlet I turned to was painting. I moved my home art studio to a new gallery space in downtown Raleigh. When I was there, I immersed myself in painting, the world of art, and becoming friends with the other tenants. I turned off the part of my brain dedicated to caregiving and allowed myself this pleasure. I would go there several days a week and always looked forward to the vibrant First Friday evenings downtown when all the galleries were open, music played, and people were out exploring. Occasionally Mark joined me on those evenings. This was the joy, the speck of light that I promised myself.

But I couldn't completely escape. One First Friday, Emily was with me at my studio, and she received a series of texts from Mark. His jaw had gotten stuck shut. He couldn't open his mouth. We rapidly locked up my studio and left. I didn't feel comfortable driving, so Emily drove us home. When we got there, Mark was in his wheelchair in the kitchen. His face was frozen in pain, and his eyes were saying, "Help me." We called 911. Two EMTs arrived, and we quickly explained what MSA was and what had happened. They took him to the ER, and we followed behind. He was lying in triage, and the nurse came in. With all of her might, she tried to open his jaw, but it wouldn't budge. They eventually gave him a heavy dose of muscle relaxant, and his jaw slackened. This was a speck of darkness in my place of light.

CHAPTER SIXTEEN

Seeking Comfort

I BEGAN SEARCHING FOR online support. I found the MSA South Atlantic USA Facebook page. I read all the comments and postings before deciding to jump in. The patients and caregivers were asking questions and revealing frustration and sadness as they battled MSA. It took some time to get the courage to join them. When I was ready, I posted, "Hi, I'm Julia and my husband has MSA."

I noticed there was another woman asking questions about doctors in the Raleigh and Durham area. Her name was Sandra, and her husband, Doug, also had MSA. I sent her an email with the subject line "hand-in-hand with MSA." Her response came an hour later. She was eager to get together to discuss our situation, from the wife's perspective. She added that they had two children. I signed off with, "We'll have so much to share."

Since we had never met, I told her I'd be wearing a purple "Cure MSA" bracelet. I picked her out as soon as she got out of her car. She had the look of worry I understood. We embraced. I plopped a tissue box on our little table. We talked for almost three hours.

It felt good to share, laugh, and cry with someone who knew exactly what I was going through. Our email exchanges over the following months were filled with names of doctors and acupuncturists, worries about changes in our husbands' health, and what to do about panic attacks. We continued to talk and meet, but our husbands never met.

I asked her what she did to get through the low days. She said she went outside at night after everyone was asleep so she could sit and look at the stars. She cried and got mad at God. She felt better the next day. Sandra emailed me the day after Doug passed away on May 17, 2013. I burst into tears when I read about his death. I had never met him but felt a connection to his life. She and I got together a few weeks after Doug's funeral at our regular place to talk about Doug and her children.

After her husband died, Sandra gave us his DynaVox, a computer that voices what you type into it. Mark's speech was changing too; his voice was becoming softer, his words slurred. While his physical decline seemed rapid, these speech changes didn't seem as obvious to me initially. When the technician arrived to show us how to use the DynaVox, Mark asked him, "Can you make me sound like Michael Caine?"

When I returned home, I asked Mark if he would like to meet Sandra. He said yes. She came to our home a couple of weeks later. The three of us spoke, laughed, and shed a few tears together. As she was leaving, Mark thanked her for coming and said: "Finally, someone from my planet."

I needed more face-to-face contact with people, like Sandra, in my same situation. To this end, I attended a local caregivers conference at the McKimmon Center on North Carolina State University's campus. The booths that filled the rooms of the conference were geared toward caregiving for senior citizens, not for younger disabled patients or their spouses. I needed a conference where I could meet someone my age.

Though the conference was not what I expected, I did have a meaningful conversation about my situation with a woman from the Guiding Lights organization, a group that focuses on families managing dementia care. I literally fell into her arms in tears. Later, she emailed me the name of a caregiver support group nearby.

I eagerly visited the Caregivers Support Group the following week but immediately realized I was in the wrong type of group. This was a room of fifty- to sixty-year-olds caring for their eighty- to ninety-year-old parents. They weren't sad. Instead, they had amusing stories about highly forgetful aging parents. One lady told a funny story about taking her mother to the same restaurant each evening for dinner. At the end of every meal, her mother would say, "I love this place. Why haven't we ever been here before? Can we come back tomorrow?" Everyone in the group laughed.

I was the last to speak. I hesitated. I thought maybe I should decline and not say anything. I thought, *Well, I'm here, I might as well see if sharing with a group of strangers is helpful.* I immediately got everyone's attention as I sobbed through my story. The group was riveted. Their eyes were solidly on me, soaking up every word. I felt on display. I was an open, bleeding cut.

After the conference and visiting this support group, I was still searching for a group that was for younger spouses caring for their unhealthy young spouses.

I found a book at a used bookstore called *Surviving Your Spouse's Chronic Illness* by Chris McGonigle. I read it in three days. It hit every nerve in my body. I related to almost every word. At the back of the book, there was a *Where to Find Help* section. That's where I discovered the Well Spouse Association (WSA). I found their website and located a chapter in the Raleigh area. I went to my first meeting shortly afterward. The association's motto is: "When one is sick . . . two need help." Truer words have never been written.

The meetings took place in a cafeteria in a large office building in Research Triangle Park. When I got there, I was greeted by a man my age waiting for me outside the building. He told me he ran the local chapter. Together, we stepped inside and made our way to a table where two women about my age were sitting. There were just the four of us that day.

Our discussion covered a variety of topics, including traveling with your disabled spouse and issues with children. I jumped in and asked for each of them to describe their ill spouse. Their stories were filled with anguish, yet they seemed to be coping. I pictured their spouses at home, managing difficult tasks of daily living while they daydreamed to escape the sadness. As the meeting drew to a close, I asked to hear their spouses' names. The air became still. The mood shifted. I saw broken hearts in their eyes. It made me teary when I said Mark's name aloud.

We had monthly meetings. The discussions we had were intimate. I heard about older children dressing, feeding, or toileting their mother or dad. We discussed ways to cope, accept, and adapt to the oddities of chronic illness. I felt and shared their loneliness, frustration, and heartache. An insight that seemed obvious, but always a good reminder, was finding ways to make your spouse feel useful. One of the members felt at times they had nothing left to give. I made a mental note. I did not want to ever deplete myself and have nothing left to give to Mark or our children.

During one of the afternoon meetings, a few of the WSA members were reminiscing about past members. Their spouses had died, so they no longer belonged to the group. The conversations went something like this:

"Remember Jane? Her husband had the brain tumor."

"How about Tom? His wife had stage four uterine cancer."

They mentioned many more names and many new diseases I never heard of before.

Everyone in the group seemed so calm (later, I learned they were all on antidepressant medications) about what they were saying. I did not have the same reaction. I felt tense hearing about so much tragedy. I couldn't help myself: when I got in the car to go home, I got the insane giggles. Laughter, like tears, can be a tension reliever. It felt surreal that I was attending such a group. I spent close to a year with this group. After a while, the discussions no longer included new information. I was ready to move on.

While I was taking care of Mark, I needed to find a way to take care of and comfort myself. I began asking my family and friends what they used to comfort themselves during difficult times. The answers I got were wide ranging but universal: sunsets, the beach, meals, hugs, family, candlelight, reading under a quilt, hot chocolate, conversations, and quiet.

My relationships with family members, friends, and new "out of the blue" people were deepening, widening, and becoming beautiful additions to my life. My cousin Clarey and I hadn't connected for decades. She began to call weekly to check up on Mark and to touch base with me. We shared the goings-on in our lives in intimate detail, building a bond. As this bond grew, we discovered we had many common interests, such as water aerobics and painting. I looked forward to her calls. Another friend, from the West Coast, whom I used to see sporadically, became a regular monthly caller. She gave me the idea of managing my anxiety by screaming in the slow lane on the highway with radio blaring. The first time I tried this, I did so with some hesitancy and quite a bit of laughter, but, over time, I really came to appreciate the release this screaming technique brought me. The support surprised me, yet I never took anyone's actions for granted. My feelings of gratitude offset my unbearable sadness of watching Mark decline.

There is a wonderful moment in the old movie *Rowing with the Wind*. It's a film about Lord Byron and Mary Shelley and her husband, Percy, during their adventures in Europe. In one scene, they are all seated in a boat in a lake surrounded by mountains. Lord Byron says something like, "Anyone know the Albanian Mountain Song?" His friends shake their heads. He proceeds to scream as loud as he can as he stands and faces the mountains. When I drove and yelled in the slow lane, I was singing my Albanian Mountain Song!

CHAPTER SEVENTEEN

Sea Glass in the Sand

SEA GLASS CAN BE found along the beaches in New England. A friend said she would find pieces in the sand as a child. Sea glass originally came from Asian fishing boats that had glass bottles hung along their sides. The glass would break off and tumble through waves of foamy ocean until it reached the shores centuries later, with soft edges, polished and beautiful. Even today, sea glass comes from broken bottles.

The vivid colors of sea glass are a wonder to a child. The pieces get collected, carried home, and placed along a windowsill or gathered in a bowl. These broken gems glisten and sparkle; there is a story within each piece. These little stars catch the sunshine as well as the moonglow.

The sea is not like air; it suspends and makes buoyant the pieces it holds. Sea glass that finds its way to shore has floated along in waters warm and icy, rough and calm. Once whole, these broken pieces are changed bit by bit from jagged shards to silky smooth treasures.

I'm on the dock in a ropy hammock looking into the gray sun at six thirty in the morning. The dock is a solid wooden platform connected to a walkway safely leading to land. It's my first overnight trip away from Mark since his diagnosis. I am on the annual summer beach trip with my book club. I glance at Leni's beach home, my book club sisters tucked inside still asleep. A little while later, people are waking up. As the sun moves up the sky, footsteps on the path make their way toward me. The conversations take form and stories are shared. Pieces of our lives glisten and sparkle. We catch each other's glow.

CHAPTER EIGHTEEN

When Life Hands You Lemons, Skip the Lemonade and Make Margaritas

OUR HOME HAD ALWAYS been a center of action, and we couldn't see why that should stop. Before our move to Raleigh from LA in 1996, I toyed with the idea of starting an event-planning business because I loved planning parties.

Our family threw all kinds of parties: birthdays, graduations, and holidays were celebrated with tremendous fun. A family favorite was our annual Hanukkah party that started the year Jeremy was born. It began with games and singing. Eventually, we included an over-the-top silly talent show. We all looked forward to what song, dance, magic trick, or other surprise talent our family and friends would come up with. For Mark and me, there was nothing better than a house filled with people, delicious food, music, games, and laughter.

I decided to continue celebrating the joys of life, even though our lives were dimmed by Mark's disease and declining health. I didn't believe it was time to live each day like it was a funeral. By focusing on planning a beautiful party, my mind could relax. I could allow myself a sense of deep pleasure and be a better caregiver to Mark. It was my way of telling Death to hold off: we're living here!

In 2012 and 2013, in addition to our annual Hanukkah party, I hosted an intimate New Year's Eve dinner, a double graduation party for Jeremy and David, and an adult pajama party for out-of-town friends; I also co-hosted a friend's fiftieth birthday party. Our thirtieth anniversary was fast approaching, and we wanted to have a party to celebrate our life together. Mark and I were married on July 4, 1982. At the same time, because of all the kindnesses from family and friends, we wanted to have a special party in their honor, so I invited everyone over for a Fourth of July and thank-you party.

I was still trying to do everything myself but realized I didn't have to do it the same way I had done it before MSA. Celebrating with family and friends was more important than using fine china and serving homemade food. I took all our small tables out into the driveway and decorated them with red checkered tablecloths sprinkled with shiny blue confetti stars. I tied red, white, and blue balloons and put them in the center of tables. I hired a food truck to serve burgers and fries and made a frozen blue margarita punch. Our dining room table was laden with fifteen grocery store pies. Instead of cooking from scratch, I gathered, hunted, and hired!

Rather than being the greeter of our guests, Mark's usual role, he sat at an outside table. Many of his friends circled Mark and tended to his needs. I circulated among our other guests in and outside our home. Our kids were in charge of the fireworks. After we ate, and it became dark, there was a dazzling and colorful display of fireworks shooting up into the sky.

CHAPTER NINETEEN

The Candlesticks

IN SEPTEMBER 2012, WE made our last trip to Mayo Clinic. Mark had completed the double-blind study. During this visit he'd been tested eight hours one day, with five hours of doctor appointments the next day to discuss his disease and the test results. The medication hadn't worked. There was no discussion of the future. At the end of those two rough days, Mark said succinctly: "There are no more tools in the tool bag for me."

Mayo Clinic is in the heart of downtown Rochester, Minnesota. The town could easily be renamed Mayo-ville. The sprawling Mayo Clinic campus is linked to hotels, restaurants, and shops through hundreds of underground and above-ground walkways. Along one of the underground walkways, placed strategically after exiting the hospital, there's a chocolate shop. Mark and I called it "What the Hell Chocolates." You've just left your doctor's appointment and gotten your diagnosis and whatever bad or good news they had to tell you, so go ahead and eat all the chocolates you want. And we did.

During most of Mark's appointments, I would walk the long hallways of the hospitals looking at the beautiful works of art covering the walls and rubbing the touchable sculptures. Other times, I'd sit and listen to the music playing in the atrium. If the weather permitted, I'd stroll the side streets and take the time to look up at the sky, bits of cloud, trees, leaves, and flowers.

At the base of one of the many hospitals is a small shop that sells items carved from wood: candlesticks, bowls, and frames. I had walked past this shop hundreds of times. Each time I walked by, a pair of wooden candlesticks caught my eye. The two candlesticks were delicately intertwined. They could be dancing or embracing. I imagined how beautiful their glow would be with lit candles.

On our last day, we passed the shop on our way to meet the taxi. I stopped momentarily and looked at the candlesticks. Mark said softly, "Would you like to have those candlesticks?"

"Yes," I said, crying as I answered.

We held each other as the shop owner carefully wrapped the candlesticks in tissue. I have them in my home now. They remind me of us. Mark and me: forever intertwined and embracing.

The candlesticks from Mayo Clinic.

CHAPTER TWENTY

Aftershocks

IT IS NIGHTTIME. I climb into bed before Mark comes into the room. The room is dark and I'm under the covers transitioning to sleep. I hear a faint noise; it's Mark on his scooter, traveling down the hall to our bedroom. I can see the black shadow of his head looming large on the ceiling as he enters our room. This shadow is surrounded by a disturbing neon green glow projected by the small green lights on top of his scooter.

He pulls up next to his side of the bed. I hear other noises: clicks and clacks of the scooter, the opening of pill bottles, the creaking of drawers opening and slamming shut. After he has taken his medications, Mark climbs into bed beside me. His body tremors, and our mattress responds like an earthquake. The shaking lasts minutes, but the minutes feel like hours. Several times, Mark stops to readjust his body. More tremors, like aftershocks, vibrate the mattress, stabbing me with fear.

CHAPTER TWENTY-ONE

No Longer Anonymous

ONE EVENING AT DUSK, I realized I needed to roll our two trash cans to the street for the next day's pickup. I didn't feel like running upstairs and changing clothes or putting my shoes on. I was wearing a sheer T-shirt and no bra with frumpy sweatpants and had hastily slipped my feet into Mark's huge shoes that were sitting by the back door. Neighbors were nowhere in sight. As you can guess, as soon as I arrived at the curb with my trash cans, a parade of people showed up!

First, Scott from across the street ran up and embraced me. He was teary and told me his son offered up Mark's name at school during a prayer service for people in ill health. Next, his wife joined us. Suddenly, my next-door neighbor Sona popped by to chat and to check on Mark.

Another couple we knew were out walking their dog and stopped to ask about Mark. A few minutes later, the mail truck pulled up, and the mailwoman asked about Mark. Mark was friendly with everyone, and everyone cared about him.

While this parade seemed to go on and on, I crossed my arms awkwardly over my breasts. I looked down and noticed Mark's oversized shoes on my feet. When I went back inside, I told Mark, "So many people care about you, they're praying for you, wishing you well and want to visit."

"I'd rather be healthy and anonymous," he answered.

DREAM: My luggage is packed. My kids drop me off at the train station in downtown Raleigh. I'm off, solo, traveling across the country by train. I have a cozy berth. I wander through the train cars and sit for endless hours in the observation deck watching the wide-open landscape. There are huge blue skies, mountains, deserts, and forests.

DREAM: Mark and I are in a car. He is at the wheel. I am in the passenger seat. His seat slowly floats back, and I bend toward the wheel in order to take it. My body becomes a flying figure like one in a Chagall painting. My feet are up, and I try to embrace the wheel.

CHAPTER TWENTY-TWO

Thanksgiving 2012

I KNEW BEFORE WE pulled out of the driveway that our Thanksgiving trip to Topsail Beach would be our last vacation as a family. I felt the tension in Mark two weeks before we traveled. He looked quietly worried the whole time. He was not happy about leaving home and going somewhere unfamiliar. He didn't want his MSA on display in front of our kids. He banged on his wheelchair in frustration. This was the only time I saw him display any kind of anger.

"We'll do whatever you want," I said.

Mark was digging in his heels. He wasn't going to budge on this issue. I felt the veins in my neck tensing up. I didn't want to enter his fear. I wondered how our children would react to the trip being canceled.

"I'm going to take an Ambien, go to bed, and we can decide in the morning," I said.

The next day, I called Jeremy and asked him to speak to his dad. Just as I had hoped, Jeremy had the magic touch with Mark and said the right words. Mark's face softened while he was on the phone. They joked.

"Traveling with me will be like the movie *Weekend at Bernie's*," Mark said.

Thirty minutes after Mark got off the phone with Jeremy, Emily showed up to help me pack the car. We threw everything in as fast as we could. Emily was lighthearted with her dad. When she heard he was not looking forward to the trip, she asked, "Didn't you say you wanted to take a trip to Las Vegas with everyone?"

"Cross that off the list," Mark replied with a laugh.

Before Mark could change his mind, we were in the car and off, Emily waving to us from our driveway. The children would join us in a few days. I was behind the wheel, and Mark was in the passenger seat. This was a major change for us. Mark had always driven whenever we went anywhere together.

Two and a half hours after leaving our home, no stops, we arrived safely at the beach house. As we pulled into the driveway, we both thought the house looked wonderful. It had beautiful, sweeping views of the Intracoastal Waterway and an elevator. I removed the luggage and food from the car and reassembled Mark's electric scooter while he waited in the passenger seat. The beach house wasn't as completely accessible as it had been advertised online. After Mark discovered he was not able to use the shower, he took a sponge bath. While getting dressed, he laughed and said, "I didn't realize *Weekend at Bernie's* was a documentary."

After I unloaded and brought everything into the house, we headed to a nearby restaurant for dinner. We used the push wheelchair for the outing. After our meal, as we began to make our way to the exit door, a man, seemingly from nowhere, came up to our table. He looked directly in my eyes and asked if he could help. I immediately thought he must have had a disabled family member, because in a blink of an eye he was assisting me with tremendous kindness. Effortlessly, he pushed Mark through the restaurant, out the door, down the ramp, and to our car.

He helped guide Mark into the passenger seat. I was grateful for his help. I was beginning to understand my limits.

The next morning, I noticed a storm outside. The clouds were almost black; the wind and rain blew against the windows. Mark informed me he wanted to return home. "You can't take a disabled person out of their environment," he insisted.

I left the room and gazed at the storm outside the massive picture window. The trees swayed and rain poured. The current of the water moved swiftly under the gray skies. Oddly, the storm calmed me.

Mark maneuvered his scooter into the family room where I was standing. He said he believed we were out of sync. My wants and needs were now different from his wants and needs. I asked him to describe my wants and needs. He believed I wanted what was in the past.

"No," I said, "I'm very present-oriented now. I'm not living in the past. But I want our present to be happy, filled with good times as a family. Today is our best day, and let's make hay while the sun shines. I want to share laughs, play games, and enjoy meals around the table with you and our children. I want to be able to stay through Saturday with the kids; I'm not even thinking about Sunday. Those are my wants and needs. What are yours?"

"To be intimate with you," he answered.

I had been going to support groups, surrounding Mark and myself with family and friends, but this was a poignant reminder. I was overlooking his most important need: to connect one-on-one with each other. To stay tethered amid the turmoil.

All five children and Doe, Mark's mother who lived in Raleigh, arrived several days later. One morning, Emily, David, and I were in the bedroom with Mark. Mark was almost dressed. Emily and David helped with his shirt and shoes. Emily placed both of her arms around Mark on one side. David hugged Mark on the other side. Mark was in the middle, the faces of both children leaned against the top of his head. The four of us were chatting about this and that while Mark was being lovingly embraced.

CHAPTER TWENTY-THREE

The Van

I SAW THE GOLD wedding band dangling around her neck before I noticed anything else. The ring glistened in the sun. A ring on a chain instantly identifies you as a widow, a woman alone. The lightest piece of jewelry, a wedding band, signifies the heaviest loss.

I wondered if I would wear Mark's wedding band on a chain around my neck.

The woman wearing it was recently widowed. Her husband had died of ALS less than a month before. She gave me a hug. She was a friend of Jenn's mother, and she had come all the way from Baltimore to Raleigh so Mark and I could purchase their wheelchair-accessible van. Included in the sale was her husband's power wheelchair.

She showed Mark and me how to use the ramp, and which button in the van does what function. Mark rolled his wheelchair up the ramp on the side of the van, then turned and rolled down.

"I'm a little disappointed; I was expecting a Porsche," Mark joked.

Mark went into the house, and I continued the tour of the van. The woman opened the hood, and I looked inside. I wasn't sure what I was supposed to look at. She showed me how to hook up the battery for the van. I could tell she was not a car person. I'm not either. I'd never viewed the inside of a hood. I felt I needed to know so much more now. The two of us wobbled through the engine inspection. When we finished, we were no longer strangers, but friends, and we walked into the house with our arms around each other.

She was passing on the vehicle that carried her husband and the wheelchair her husband sat in. It was a purchase I never imagined I would make. This was not a dream car; it was a short-term purchase. I already knew before I even backed it out of the driveway there would come a day when I would sell it. I wondered who the next owner would be.

We told our children and friends they could use the van anytime they wanted to take Mark places. This allowed Mark to get out of the house and have separate experiences from me. It felt healthy and mutually respectful to be apart a little each day. With Mark not working, these outings with family and friends were essential to his emotional well-being. When Mark would return home, we could share our day's adventures just like we had when he worked. This kept us feeling like husband and wife. I didn't want to be a mother to Mark or just his caregiver. Personal and private space was still vital for both of us.

Other accessible items arrived in our home: a recliner lift chair, a stair lift to get to the second floor, handrails, scooters, travel and electric wheelchairs, ramps in doorways. They allowed Mark to have options and gave him a safe way to travel and move about our home.

Being slightly overwhelmed with just the moment-to-moment needs and demands of taking care of Mark, I pretty much abandoned my usual standards for living and decided to stop using dishes and silverware. Paper and plastic were more manageable, less demanding, and just another sign that ease was more important than elegance. Like the handrails and ramps, the paper goods were another way to simplify my life and conserve my energy. I asked David to pick up paper plates, bowls, and cups, as well as plastic utensils and coffee stirrers: a thousand of each. He had a fun day at Walmart!

With wheelchairs, lifts, paper goods, and help, I felt like I was getting a firmer grasp on managing our new lives. Mark loved the normalcy of the everyday routine, or as my friend calls it, "the blessed routine." With all the mechanical devices and outside help, we were able to keep the conversations, laughter, and tears flowing. Living and loving was more important than anything else.

The path from working to not working, walking unaided to walking with a cane, then eventually giving up the cane for a walker and finally a wheelchair, was not gradual or gentle. It was more like an avalanche of decline. As depressing as it was, Mark never gave up his positive and sometimes funny spirit.

Me: "How was your day?"

Mark: "Just another day in paradise."

CHAPTER TWENTY-FOUR

Contrasts

MARK IS GANDHI. I'M Sylvia Plath.

Mark is Nelson Mandela. I'm Margaret Thatcher on a bad hair day.

Mark is the Dalai Lama. I'm Sybil with the sixteen personalities.

He can be joy and I can be fear.

Mark didn't volunteer for his latest identity. Ironically, his truest self emerged through his illness. One morning, while dressing Mark, I tried to pull his tighter-than-hell compression socks up his calf as he sat on his scooter. I pulled too hard, and in a flash, the scooter and Mark tipped over onto the floor. I heard a soft yell from Mark as he began falling.

It was a ridiculous calamity. I struggled to untangle Mark from the scooter and pulled the scooter upright. I leaned over to examine Mark. He slowly rolled onto his back and responded, cool as a cucumber.

"While I'm down here," he said, "I might as well do my stretches."

PART

III

 END STAGE:
A LOT OF GOODBYES

CHAPTER TWENTY-FIVE

Hospice on My Speed Dial

I RECEIVED A PHONE call from hospice, asking whether Mark and I would like to arrange a meeting at our home or at their facility. I was surprised by the call. Mark had not told me about his recent appointment with his internist, where they had discussed hospice care. My immediate reaction was: *Oh crap, we're nearing the hospice zone.*

After hanging up, I decided I'd go by myself and not tell Mark where I was going.

My plan was to get all the information during that first appointment and explain it all to Mark. I felt slightly nauseated driving to hospice. It was surreal going there.

Hospice of Wake County (now called Transitions LifeCare) is a lovely and inviting campus set on a hill in southwest Raleigh. There are several brick buildings surrounded by manicured gardens with benches. Situated in the center of the circular driveway is a pleasing metal sculpture of soaring ribbonlike shapes. I waited a few minutes in a foyer. I noticed how spotless and cheery everything was around me. The colorful wall art was set against warm neutral furnishings.

The hospice administrator, Gwen, and I spoke for more than two hours. She was delightful, caring, and clear in her explanations of their protocol. I received a lot of information and realized hospice was a safe harbor. Gwen said Mark and I and our children would be assigned a team to educate and console us. The team would consist of a nurse, social worker, chaplain, and physical therapist. The whole family would be encircled. I felt different on the drive home; I was no longer anxious but relieved. I didn't have to do this alone. We now had partners and guides to help us through whatever was ahead.

A few days later, we had a home visit. Mark was able to ask his own questions. He had three concerns: first, he wanted to know if he would be able to continue using antibiotics if he got an infection; second, their opinion on feeding tubes; and third, if our internist could remain as Mark's doctor. Shortly after this visit with hospice, our internist visited us in our home and assured us he'd remain Mark's physician if we chose to join hospice.

Joining hospice is a process of acceptance. We weren't ready to accept that Mark was close to dying. So we waited. A few months later, I visited again with Emily. I needed her support and opinion. When Emily got teary during our meeting, I felt a pang of worry; perhaps I shouldn't have asked her to come with me. When we finished our conversation, we had a tour of the grounds, buildings, and in-care facility, the Hospice Home. Emily agreed with me that everything about hospice was cheerful and had a relaxed feeling.

The most coincidental thing happened during our tour. We were being shown a small sitting room with two chairs and a window overlooking a garden. In the room was a striking three-foot-tall V-shaped glass vase with a few handfuls of brightly colored pieces of sea glass resting on the bottom. I asked about the vase and stones. I was told each piece of sea glass represented a patient who had died. When the vase fills to the top, the staff creates a mosaic and places the shimmering handiwork in the garden. Emily and I immediately glanced at each other and recounted my trip to Leni's beach house and how these little iridescent pieces of broken glass symbolized a person's spirit.

Mark's physical abilities were changing, and I wanted to move us forward with hospice care. At this point, I was the one dressing Mark in the morning and undressing him at night. He was weakening and becoming more fragile. I was becoming drained trying to do all the caregiving. Yet, it was hard to let go of the role and let a stranger step in to do much of the day-to-day intimate care. Another month or so passed before we found the courage to at last sign the papers for our hospice admission.

I was so drained the day we signed with hospice, I went to bed before eight o'clock. Yet I was restless. I churned and turned from side to side. I swung my legs on top of the blankets and back under. I couldn't get comfortable. I repositioned myself, looked out the window at the darkness. I scrolled through Facebook, glanced at emails, started reading a book, then closed it. I skipped around YouTube music videos trying to find the right song that would help me sleep and wondered what the kids were doing. I stayed in bed, eventually falling asleep, waking again at eight in the morning.

It was the start of winter when hospice first called, and spring when we at last signed. The time between winter and spring stretched out uncomfortably between the two of us. I felt like I was swimming through molasses, and everything was in slow motion, while, for Mark, things were moving too fast in his decline.

I added hospice as a new contact in my phone. By summer, Mark and I were allowing the experience and relationship with hospice to happen and grow. There was now a steady flow of new faces and personalities in our lives; the nurse, nurse's aide, social worker, physical therapist, and chaplain were regular visitors to our home. Mark never went to live at the Hospice Home, but I was no longer the primary caregiver. The hospice staff, who were once strangers, had now joined us on our journey and felt like friends.

The hospice team were down-to-earth, and their conversations were matter-of-fact. They sat comfortably in a chair near Mark when speaking with him and always listened to what he said. They maintained steady eye contact and were ready with a warm smile and a laugh. They never rushed a conversation. The discussions they had with us about dying were ordinary conversations. They were teaching me how to talk about living and dying in a natural way. There was no taboo. Nothing was off-limits.

During our first visit with the physical therapist, she asked, "How does the end look?" I didn't understand what she was asking, but Mark knew. He answered as if he'd been asked about the weather.

"Infection, pulmonary embolism, heart attack, or respiratory failure."

After she left, I asked him if that was hard to answer.

"No," he said, "but maybe my answer should have been 'Bullet to the head or throwing myself out the window.'"

Many people on the hospice staff had begun their career with newborns, later switching career paths to dying patients. Initially, I didn't see the correlation. Soon, it became crystal clear. Did these people have an affinity to the life cycle? Were they drawn to the mystery of beginnings and endings of life? There are huge unknowns and infinite darkness at both ends. There is hard labor prior to birth and hard labor before death. There are ways to breathe and medicate in nearing death, just as there are ways to facilitate birthing through breathing and medications. There are things you can control, but mostly things you cannot control. The rhythm slows, then rushes. You have to let go, then embrace. We are often taught throughout life to push ourselves to succeed and advance past all obstacles. However, death requires the development of an entirely new skill:

letting go of our life and loved ones. We have to let go of everything and find peace in order to die in peace.

One morning, when the nurse's aide from hospice had arrived to help with Mark, I left to go swimming. I was by myself in the indoor pool. The hazy sunlight streaked into the room through the windows. I spotted leaf-covered branches swaying in all directions. I didn't swim or do laps. Like the branches, I spun around in the water, chopping it with my arms and legs. I pushed and pulled the water with my hands, reached up and flung my arms, bent my fingers, raised my knees, twisted my hips, then dove to touch the bottom of the pool and heard odd echo sounds while underneath.

CHAPTER TWENTY-SIX

Mark's Team of Angels

INCLUDED IN "MARK'S TEAM" from hospice was a certified nurse assistant (CNA) who arrived each morning to help. This included personal hygiene, administering medication, and getting Mark dressed. Initially, I did the remaining caregiving for the rest of the day and evening. Fairly quickly, I felt my patience wane; I needed more help. I reminded myself I wanted to be Mark's wife, not his full-time caregiver. Mark agreed, and eventually we hired CNAs outside of hospice to help us from 10:30 a.m. to 9:30 p.m. each day. Our insurance benefits helped pay for the additional help. They were patient and professional and always smiled. I referred to everyone who helped Mark as "Mark's Angels."

It was an adjustment for everyone in our family to have a caregiving professional in our home all the time. The CNAs, however, knew when to step in and when to step aside if family or friends were present. For them to feel comfortable in our home and be able to do their jobs, I had to let go of the private spaces in our home: the kitchen and Mark's and my bathroom and bedroom. It no longer mattered to me which pan or bowl was used for cooking soup or how they assembled the toiletries in our bathroom or straightened our bed. What mattered was I had another pair of gentle hands assisting Mark, and I could once again be his wife. These are excerpts from conversations I had with them.

BINTA IS FROM THE GAMBIA AND DESCRIBED WORKING WITH MARK:

I'm his hands and feet. Yet I let him make his own decisions. I have to feel what my patients are feeling in order to help them. My job is not to think about their illness but to enjoy the day with my patient. My gift is laughter and to become friends with my patient. The first week I'm in a patient's home, I study the person and family. I invaded their privacy by entering their home. I want the patient to be comfortable around me. The best thing a family can do is to love and encourage their loved one and let them be involved with decisions. I'm continually learning something new in my job.

Mark is very patient with himself and me. His demands are low. He is kind, positive, and brave. He thinks about why the doctors do not have a cure for MSA.

HERE IS WHAT ABI HAD TO SAY ABOUT BEING A CNA:

I feel you can go through the training to become a CNA, but if you don't have empathy and compassion for what you do to help a patient, you cannot care for people. Each morning I pray for myself, my patients, and their families. I pray for their good health and their ability to cope with the challenges they face.

When I work with younger terminally ill people like Mark, they are often angry and rage-full. Mark, on the other hand, handles his situation gracefully. The first day I met Mark, I felt deeply for him; his age was the exact age as my mother. I considered being removed from Mark, worried it could become too painful to watch him decline. I decided to stay. Mark made me laugh. I never saw him angry. He talked about how good his life has been. I could see he loved his wife and children. He said it was their love that kept him going.

PAT ARRIVED IN OUR HOME IN THE EVENINGS:

It is a blessing to be able to work and another blessing to be allowed into people's homes when they know nothing about you. Anytime a family allows me in their home, I feel honored. They don't have to choose me.

There are some situations with a patient that are really hard, and some that are easy. I take all the jobs. It wouldn't be fair to turn down a job because it was going to be hard. Everyone deserves the chance to be taken care of in the right way.

I start the first day of every job with a prayer. I stand outside the person's home and ask God to show me the correct way to provide care for my new patient I know nothing about. I pray for signs to show me understanding. You can't be trained for what you're about to walk into.

I can read people's facial expressions. I have a sense about people. I can look around their home; their things tell a story. I watch the family and can get an even better sense about my patient. I try and keep the person as close to who they were before their illness.

Right away, after meeting Mark, I knew how much Mark loved Julia and his children.

Mark didn't expect to get MSA. He doesn't question what happened; he sees it as a random event. It happened, and he's dealing with it and taking it to somewhere inspirational. He is still living his life to the fullest he can.

He's an inspiration to his family. It doesn't matter that he sits in a chair. His family looks up to him, loves, admires, and respects him. Old Dad and new Dad, it's the same to them. They see Dad, not the disease. They don't doubt he is their dad.

On the other hand, Mark feels emotional pain at not being who he was before the disease. The hardest part for Mark is within himself. He is so smart and driven. He is used to doing for everyone else and getting it all done. He misses his old self.

He's never going to show his internal pain fully. He's protecting Julia and his children. We're seeing 75 percent of Mark's emotions. The other 25 percent he's keeping to himself. That is Mark. He's always been the protector and will always be to the end.

The old Mark knew no limits. He reached for the sky, and no matter how high the sky was, he could touch it. He had no limitations. The limitations he has now are in the 25 percent. The 25 percent is where he struggles.

At first, being a CNA was a job, and it still is. But I think about myself when I see a family struggle with death. This job humbles me and has made me a better person, not a perfect person. I take care of people in their home. Afterward, I carry it outside in the world, and it makes you care for people in society.

I ride the roller coaster along with the family. I have cried with the family. It's an honor to meet Mark, Julia, Jeremy, Jenn, Emily, James, and David.

KESSIE IS ORIGINALLY FROM GHANA. THIS IS WHAT SHE HAD TO SAY ABOUT MARK:

Mark is unique. He's not just thinking of him, him, him. He thinks mostly about Julia and his children. He's asked me several times: How do I think Julia and the children will do after I'm gone?

He has not let the disease take control of his life. He's not depressed; he pushes himself, and he has had stronger days.

There is a big difference when a family keeps loving and encouraging the patient.

I told Mark he will see Emily's baby. He answered, "Yes, I'm hoping for that."

There was a poignant moment when Mark asked me, "How will you feel when you do something for me and I can't say thank you?"

I answered him: some facial expressions say it all.

CHAPTER TWENTY-SEVEN

Managing the Caregiving Marathon

CAREGIVING FOR A LOVED one with MSA or any terminal illness is like running a marathon, not a sprint. At my best, I kept a relaxed pace because I could see the miles before me. There wasn't a sense of rushing. I deliberately chose the turtle's pace, not the hare's. I had miles to go. Doing too much too early can risk burnout.

My advice for anyone doing this: Take breaks and catch your breath even though you might think you don't have time for yourself. Take it. Eat healthy but also indulge your sweet tooth. You will feel even better! Be forgiving of yourself. You're doing something you've never done before. Laugh every day.

MY FAVORITE SURVIVAL TIPS:

- Keep ice cream in the fridge and candy on the counter.

- Wear comfy clothes but not pajamas. Getting dressed helped me not get depressed.

- Let in as much light as possible. There were days I knew I wouldn't get outside. I needed that sunshine to keep me going.

- Bring a moment of joy to the end of the day. I installed white twinkle lights on my deck. I loved turning on those lights and having a cup of hot chocolate on my deck alone.

CHAPTER TWENTY-EIGHT

Screwdrivers and Sparkles!

OUR CURTAIN ROD NEEDED tightening, and I had no idea how to fix it. Mark explained patiently which screwdriver to use and how to tighten the rod. He watched and guided me from his scooter. He also explained how to pay the bills, change the water filter every six months in the refrigerator when the light turns purple, and how Social Security works. I didn't want to know these things. He reminded me there were many people in my life I could turn to.

I only wanted to turn to him.

I resisted opening the bills for a long time. Mark instinctively knew what this change in our jobs would mean, and he waited for me to feel ready. I didn't want to know how to pay them. Mark always paid the bills. In the past, when the mail arrived, I'd pull out the party invitations and hand the rest of the mail to Mark.

I shared my reluctance to learn about bill paying with my friend Tracy while I visited at her home. She offered to teach me. I knew I was turning a corner when I asked about her bill-paying system. We walked into her home office, and she showed me her file cabinets and folders. She told me what to purchase and said she'd start coming to our house, with Mark seated nearby, and guide me.

I could take in her words. In contrast, I was walled off from Mark teaching me. I would get upset whenever he talked about it. He wasn't the reason for my resistance. It was the changing dynamic in our lives. If I started paying the bills, I would be doing his job since he wasn't physically capable. That realization was painful.

Finally, I was ready. I went to an office supply store by myself, got a cart, and strolled up and down each aisle. I selected a twelve-month folder for the monthly bills exactly like the one Tracy had. I viewed the stacking trays. There were so many options. I picked the clear acrylic ones. I saw brightly colored glitter stickers of butterflies, flowers, and flamingos and ones with cute words: "happy," "smile," "friends," and "celebrate." I decided I had to make this bill-paying thing playful and creative. I bought a dozen packets of these decorative and fun stickers.

I continued my shopping spree and bought brightly colored pens, fluorescent paper clips and rubber bands, a pink stapler, pencil holders with sparkles, and pencils with purple feathers on the ends. I was getting excited now. When I returned home, I immediately covered all the folders, file cabinets, and stacking trays with the glitter stickers! I told Mark, if I make my bill paying glittery and attractive, the colors will catch my eye, and I'll remember to pay the bills.

Learning to pay our bills became an intimate and challenging experience. Tracy and I would be side by side at my makeshift sparkle-covered desk while Mark sat near us answering our questions. The first day Tracy arrived to help me, Mark directed us to open the computer so we could go to our bank's website.

"Does everyone pay bills by opening a bank site?" I asked. Mark and Tracy both laughed.

Each bill is a story, I tell Mark. They represent our medical life, social life, work life. I can now look at an envelope and detect what's inside. There are envelopes offering promise: free gifts, rewards, and ways to beat the market. Other envelopes make no attempt at all to win you over, by having no promises anywhere, only a typed address and name. Those envelopes offer just a cold stare. I learned to decipher sneaky bill-like sales techniques: bills that are not bills but are made to look like bills. Or checks made out in my name, ready to be cashed or deposited. Ha! You can't fool me anymore.

The entire plot of the 2013 movie *Nebraska* centered on an elderly man named Woody who had been duped into thinking he won a million-dollar sweepstakes prize. It was a mail scam. Woody was willing to walk to Lincoln, Nebraska, from Billings, Montana, to collect his winnings. Could this have been me? Fortunately, Tracy and Mark were there with me helping to interpret this new language.

Jeremy also helped explain finances to me one evening. I was having difficulty understanding what he was telling me. He ran up to our board game closet and brought down the Game of Life. He took out the little buildings, paper money, and tiny pink and blue people and laid out everything on the kitchen table. One building represented our home, another, the Wells Fargo bank. He made a short pile of money with a little blue figure on top. The little figure represented our financial adviser who manages our investments. He continued by laying flat the stock cards and minivan with our family riding inside. He knew just what to do to make me laugh and help me get through one piece of my new life.

CHAPTER TWENTY-NINE

Next

I COULDN'T LEAVE MARK for long on his own and was barely able to go to my downtown art studio to work. I was torn. I was paying rent for the studio and loved being among the other artists. But Mark was home, and I needed to be close to him. So, after two years, I decided to close my studio.

I worried I was leaving my life as an artist behind. One of the other artist tenants, Lea, assured me, "Julia, you'll move forward. Even on your knees or belly, you'll be moving forward."

I wasn't emotionally able to take down the art from the walls and remove all my supplies. I felt heartbroken. I couldn't do it. My children, Debbie (James's mother), and Mike (James's brother) did it for me. They loaded everything in a few cars and unloaded it at my house. I stood in the kitchen, wiping the counters as they briskly walked through the house with boxes of my things and carried them up the stairs to my home studio. My life as an artist was on hold.

At one point, Jenn walked by me carrying a painting. We made eye contact, and I said, "Next! Something new will take its place." She smiled and went back for another painting.

That evening, we celebrated Jeremy's birthday. During dinner, Jenn and Jeremy announced to us they were expecting a baby in September! The "Next" had arrived.

CHAPTER THIRTY

The Misheberach

DAVID AND I WERE guests at a bar mitzvah. During the service, the rabbi mentioned Mark's name in the prayer for healing, the Misheberach. This is said during every service and literally means "May the One who blesses, bless those in need of healing."

It should not have surprised us to hear Mark's name called out. Tears sprang into both our eyes. I held David's hand. The prayer was an emotional release for us.

It was a moment when I realized all of us needed healing.

CHAPTER THIRTY-ONE

The Graduations

DAVID AND JEREMY GRADUATED from UNC–Chapel Hill over the same weekend in May 2013. Jeremy's law school ceremony was on Saturday, and David's undergraduate ceremony was held the following day.

Mark wanted to be there, but both graduations were scheduled to start around eleven. To get seats, we were told we needed to be there by ten, which meant leaving our house at the latest by nine. There was no way Mark could be ready to leave so early, so the children and I decided we would attend without him.

Mark's friend Chris offered to stay with Mark during the graduations. Our son-in-law James stayed with Mark as well. It was decided beforehand that if Mark suddenly felt strong enough, the two of them could assist Mark, get him dressed and ready and into the van, and James would drive Mark to the graduation.

I was sitting with Emily, David, and Jenn and her parents at the basketball stadium where Jeremy's graduation was to take place. The ceremony had already begun. Suddenly, David received a text message. Mark and

James were on their way! David jumped up and went to meet them just outside the stadium.

As I turned to my right, there was Mark, riding into the ceremony in his electric wheelchair, with James and David walking on either side. At the moment Mark came into the stadium, Jeremy happened to look up, and their eyes met. Moments later, Mark wheeled up next to me, and we were able to watch Jeremy receive his diploma together.

The next day was déjà vu all over again. Chris and James stayed with Mark at the house until Mark felt he had enough strength to make the trip to Chapel Hill. Once again, Mark pushed himself to get dressed and ready for David's graduation. This time, the ceremony was taking place on the football field. As the ceremony began, Emily, Jeremy, Jenn, and I sat together, hoping to receive James's text message that he and Mark were on their way.

Jeremy got the text and met James and Mark outside. They accompanied Mark as he wheeled himself through the tunnel and onto the football field. David, who was sitting with his classmates in the bleachers, saw Mark immediately. We were overjoyed both days and afterward celebrated with a beautiful party in our home.

CHAPTER THIRTY-TWO

Revealing Ourselves

JEREMY, EMILY, AND DAVID assisted their dad and me in so many ways. They ran errands, drove their dad to doctor appointments, picked up medicines and meals, and listened to our concerns. To thank them for all they had done, I decided to take our children on a wonderful trip. It was time to nurture the caregivers. I wanted to spend time with them one-on-one.

Mark agreed this was a great idea. Mark's brother, Richard, offered to stay with Mark in our home while I was away. I found a resort on the beach in Miami and booked rooms for seven nights. My plan was to have each of the children spend three nights with me. David flew down with me. Emily, the second to join me, overlapped with David for one night. Jeremy, overlapping with Emily for one night, arrived at the end of my stay.

David and I saw the resort for the first time together and explored every part of the beautiful property. We quickly hopped into an outdoor Jacuzzi, and afterward, I swam a few laps in the nearby pool while David took off for a boxing class. And that was the week: deciding which class to take and where to have lunch and dinner. At each meal I made a toast, thanking them for all they had done and continued to do for their dad. The meals were leisurely. In the spirit of following their lead, I followed the direction they wanted our conversations to go.

David, the youngest, spoke primarily about his past. He had just graduated from college and was at the start of his adulthood. We reminisced a lot. He had hilarious memories of middle school and high school. He spoke about travels through Europe, studying at the University of Pittsburgh and UNC–Chapel Hill.

Emily often kept the conversation to the present. She asked directly about what funeral plans we had decided on. She wanted to help with phone calls and be responsible for taking care of our wishes. Emily also spoke about becoming a mother in the future and missing Dad at that time.

Jeremy, our eldest, spoke about the future. One night at dinner, Jeremy said he felt our relationship would head in a new direction. He said he thought we would become closer. He offered to do the things Dad would do or advise. He wondered if I had plans to sell our house. He mentioned there was a tax break if I sold the house within two years after becoming a widow. That is something Mark would have considered. We talked about Jeremy becoming a father, and what a fantastic grandfather Mark would have been—full of fun ideas no one else would have conjured up.

Though I could see what lay ahead with MSA, I worried about the emotional storm I feared would plow into the children and me after losing Mark. This was subconsciously weighing on my mind as the week progressed. Emily arrived late Thursday; David was scheduled to leave early the following morning.

I was just getting into my pajamas when I suddenly began crying. My chest and throat tightened and felt on fire. My first thought was to call Mark and ask him what I should do. I quietly shut my bedroom door. I didn't want David and Emily to hear me. I didn't know if I was having a heart attack, a panic attack, or both. I picked up my phone. It was past midnight. I knew Mark was asleep. I didn't know who else to call. He would know exactly what to do. I texted him, "Up?" I waited anxiously, adding, "Asleep?" My crying increased. I called him on the home phone. When he picked up, I blurted out, "I don't know what to do. Should I go to the hospital? Am I having a heart attack or an anxiety attack?"

Mark, calm as always, asked a few questions to rule out a heart attack.

"It's probably anxiety," he said. "I'm not there. You need to go to Emily and David. They're not kids; they're adults. They can help you. I can't. I'm not there. Keep me on speakerphone."

I didn't want to leave my room and be sad in front of Emily and David. But I trusted Mark's advice, opened the door of my room, and stepped into the sitting room. I stood there in front of them crying.

"I think I'm having an anxiety attack," I said.

They both leapt up and embraced me. Mark was on speakerphone. He listened.

They jumped in with words of comfort and understanding. They easily addressed the obvious issues of me panicking because of their father's illness and the stress his illness had added to my life. They pointed out it was my first trip away from him in a long time and I was missing him. Once I had calmed down, they steered the conversation toward something funny.

David mentioned I had taken six exercise classes that day. My body was on overload! Mark could hear us all laughing. The shifting of roles is part of the package you receive along with the diagnosis of a chronic illness. Shifting roles turned out to be an unexpected gift.

Jeremy was with me on the last day of the trip. A storm was making its way to the coast. The clouds were dark, the wind blowing. I was drawn to being outside. Jeremy and I found two cushioned lounge chairs near the ocean. I couldn't take my eyes off the sky and clouds. The ocean was choppy and gray. The palm trees swayed and made a whooshing sound. I noticed many people heading indoors, but I wanted to stay outside in the storm. Raindrops began landing on us. Even after spotting lightning, we remained outdoors for as long as we could.

CHAPTER THIRTY-THREE

Shifts

MARK WAS FORCED BY his illness to relinquish his independence. He was a self-made man. He had started several businesses from the ground up and was successful each time. In Los Angeles, he had been a consultant to doctors and hospitals. When he sold that business, Mark was looking for a change. We began reading articles about Raleigh as a fast-growing and exciting city. We made the plunge and moved to North Carolina in 1996. He opened a business as an executive recruiter for health insurance companies.

Before MSA, Mark had felt freedom all around him. As it progressed, our world shrank to the confines of our home. We had never spent so much time indoors, day and night, along with our steady flow of visitors and nurse's aides.

Before MSA, I was content being an artist and stay-at-home mother and was unbothered by being dependent on Mark. Now, I was forced to give up my dependency on him. It was not at all what I thought my life would be at this moment. I saw our shifting roles and transformations like movements in a dance. Mark was always beside me, holding and caring for me. I felt free because of him being there. Now my dance was no longer a *pas de deux*. I found myself cautiously moving solo, finding my footing while holding onto the thin branches of support he was still able to offer.

CHAPTER THIRTY-FOUR

Goodbyes

"WE NEED TO TALK," Mark said one day. I braced myself.

"I'm worse and weaker than I've ever been," he continued tearfully. "I now need help to do basic personal hygiene. I don't want intervention; I want to let the disease take its natural course. Let the dying happen. I love you, Julia, and have loved our life together."

Mark began to advise me on how I should live after he was gone. He said I should sell the house and move on. He said there would be ghosts in our house. I answered maybe I wanted those ghosts. I told him I might want to see the exact spots where he and I and our kids had meals together, washed dishes, sat on the deck, and had coffee in the evenings. I told him I didn't know if I could leave those memories. Those spots could become sacred. I wasn't sure what to do about our house.

Mark looked the weakest I'd ever seen. I knew he must have been thinking, *I'm dying, and I could die right now.* He was suffering and at times seemed to be saying, "I'm done."

As he spoke to me about what he felt I should do, we both cried. He was worried about me being alone. He hoped friends would move in with me for a bit after he passed. He said my life was heading in a new direction and he wanted me to know, as strange and weird as it sounded, that I should even allow another intimate relationship into my life, if that's what I wanted. We held each other a long time, stroking cheeks and hair, arms and hands. We looked into each other's eyes as if we were trying to memorize them.

During one of my visits with the hospice chaplain, I asked her how I should say goodbye to Mark and whether it was something important for me to do. I wanted to know if it could be wordless, a hug, a kiss, something other than spoken words. I couldn't imagine saying goodbye without falling to pieces. Would I regret not saying goodbye? I knew if I did it would be an ugly cry. On the other hand, maybe Mark would want to see my sadness. Sometimes I hid my sadness in order not to cause him additional pain.

If I said goodbye too early, would Mark throw in the towel and let go of life, become weaker and pass away, figuring the goodbyes have been said? I continued asking questions. After saying an emotional goodbye, how do you say it's time to eat dinner?

I had been grieving Mark for years. It haunted me to wonder how long I had left with him. I spoke about all this with the chaplain. It was like a dress rehearsal, saying it out loud with her first, hearing how it sounded and what it felt like to say goodbye.

I assumed it would be weeks before I broached the subject. That night, however, after eating almost an entire box of chocolate-covered marshmallow cookies, I decided to express all my feelings to Mark in bed.

"Do you remember after the diagnosis, I said I want you in any shape? And you said, 'Julia, be careful what you wish for.' It's been two years since those words were spoken, and I still want you, in this shape or any shape. I can see you and look into your eyes. I can sleep beside you and talk with you, sharing all my worries and thoughts."

I thanked him for being a wonderful husband and father and my best friend. He was someone who made me feel safe. "I cannot imagine living without you," I said. "Who will I feel connected to? When you're not here, you will be the only person I would want to comfort me. I wonder if I will roll up into a ball. I wonder if I will be okay? I will think of you every day. I will miss you every day."

We cried and held each other. We told each other "I love you" over and over again.

Mark said our family would pull together. He added that we would have had so much fun with our grandchildren. I cried imagining Mark surrounded by our grandchildren and them loving him so much. How could it be possible they won't know him?

"Don't let go because I said goodbye," I told him.

I added a few moments later, "Any secrets you want to tell me?"

Mark responded, "I've been an open book. You know everything about me."

A week later, we had another visit with the chaplain. Mark brought up the topic of funeral arrangements and his obituary. Bam! I thought: *Mark feels his end is imminent.*

While Mark openly discussed the details of what he wanted for his funeral, I listened. The chaplain said she had known some people who wrote their own obituary or had one of their children write it ahead of time. The conversation flowed. Then, there was a silence.

I asked Mark whether he was scared of anything.

"When I pass, I won't know. I'll be in a casket," he said.

Mark said he tried not to think about what he'd miss in the future. It made him too sad to think about not seeing our children go through their adult lives and not being a part of our grandchildren's lives.

While Mark spoke, he didn't take his eyes off me.

There was another silence for a few minutes. Then the chaplain asked me: "Julia, what are you scared of?"

I didn't expect to cry. But I did for several minutes. I said: "I'm doing okay now because Mark is here. I see him each day. We laugh and talk. I can ask him questions and get his advice. I'm scared when he won't be here. I'll be strong. I know life goes on. It's an awful thing to figure out how to be okay."

The chaplain nodded.

Mark said, "We're in each other's bones."

CHAPTER THIRTY-FIVE

Funeral Arrangements

ONE AFTERNOON, I WAS walking up our driveway, and Emily, David, and Jeremy happened to be standing there talking.

"I'm going to the cemetery in the next few weeks to select plots," I blurted out. "Anyone want to come? Any takers?"

A few silent seconds went by.

"I'll go," Jeremy said.

Emily and David followed: "I'll go."

A few days later, while Jeremy and I were driving together to pick up something for Mark, Jeremy said, "How about if just the two of us go?"

"That's fine," I answered.

A trip to the cemetery is not exactly a group activity.

A few weeks later, Jeremy and I drove to the cemetery, near Chapel Hill, and found the right place for Mark and me to be buried.

Our friends provided comfort and support in surprising ways. One of our friends, Jonathan, assisted me with Mark's funeral arrangements. This was important to Mark. He wanted to know that the details were taken care of ahead of time. We both agreed the kids didn't need to assist me with these arrangements.

Initially, Mark asked to be in on the email loop regarding the funeral. He was curious and would ask Jonathan about the different packages we could buy. The conversations we had over the funeral arrangements went something like this:

Mark: Julia, do you want the limo?

Me: I think so. I don't think I'll be in the mood to drive that day.

Eventually, Mark asked to be taken off the email loop between Jonathan and me.

The day Jonathan and I had our appointment to go to the funeral home to sign and pay, I told Mark I had a few errands to run. I popped a Xanax and met Jonathan in a nearby parking lot, and he drove the rest of the way. I quickly learned that funeral homes are far from homey. We were led into a room to sign papers. It was a large room full of caskets. The room certainly didn't put me at ease. Dozens of caskets in every style and color hung from every inch of wall space.

Sitting there was weird, funny, sad, and strange all at once. Jonathan did most of the talking while I tried *not* looking at the caskets. I answered a couple of questions, but having to say Mark's birthday and full name was difficult. Instead, I wrote the answers on a scrap of paper and slid the paper toward the woman assisting us.

I signed and initialed many papers and paid for everything with a credit card.

Their all-business approach was intentional and drained the emotions out of the transaction. I might as well have been placing a large order for doughnuts.

The experience left me feeling cold. They were the ones who knew what they were doing, right? What type of room would have been more inviting? Definitely a room without caskets. Was there a way to soften the blow of paying for your husband's funeral in advance? Certainly. But I don't know what that would be.

That evening in bed, I said simply, "Jonathan and I took care of everything today. It's done."

The Provider

MARK WAS ALWAYS A protector, provider, and planner. He had confidence in his role in all the areas of his life: son, brother, friend, businessman, husband, and father. Shortly after his diagnosis in 2011, Mark stopped working. He filed a claim for benefits from the insurance company where he had bought a disability policy thirty years earlier, long before there was any hint he might ever need it. He bought it because he was self-employed and had to be sure, no matter what happened, he could provide for his family. At the time he bought the policy, we were newly married and had two small children, and Mark was moving forward with a new career. He was in perfect health, and so was I.

When he first filed the claim, the insurance company stonewalled. Mark, with his usual tenacity, fought for two years with an attorney to receive his benefits as promised by the disability policy. For those two years, until the disability benefits kicked in, we lived off savings. Those benefits are what helped us pay for the additional CNA help.

MSA is a disease that usually strikes people in their late forties and early fifties. This is during their prime earning years. In our midfifties, Mark and I were suddenly facing a triple crisis: health, emotional, and financial.

Mark was terrified about lack of income. Eventually, we received the benefits, and Mark and I lived off monthly insurance payments from the disability policy. This included a six-month widow's benefit after Mark passed away. Without the disability policy, our financial outcome would have been totally different. Having watched this unfold, our married children have made sure to have these types of policies included in their work benefits packages.

CHAPTER THIRTY-SEVEN

The Mandala

MARK AND I WERE walking around Sausalito, California, in 2001, on our way to get an ice cream cone when we passed an art gallery with a mandala hanging in the window. Mark was fascinated by it. While we were eating ice cream, he kept going back to the gallery to look at it, and then he bought it! He liked to say it was the most expensive ice cream he'd ever eaten.

The mandala is a large seven-by-seven-foot tapestry, adorned with circles within circles. Within the many circles are squares within squares. It is brightly colored with warm oranges, pinks, yellows, blues, and greens. There are flowers, leaves, objects that appear to be trees, architectural designs, and vessels that could be human figures. There is balance and symmetry within the colors, shapes, and lines.

Mandalas have multiple interpretations and are used for different purposes. The Swiss psychologist Carl Jung viewed the mandala as a representation of "the Self, the wholeness of the personality, which if all goes well is harmonious."[6] Within Buddhist philosophy, one can make a mandala offering, and if our minds are open, we will receive a teaching. If we receive a teaching, we can transform negative circumstances into positive ones. One afternoon, the chaplain came to our home, and we stood in front of the mandala tapestry. I told her of the serenity and peace the object brought to me. I talked about the labyrinth I walked at Mayo Clinic the day after Mark's diagnosis. I remembered the paths I walked in Saugatuck, Michigan, while attending painting classes at Oxbow.

There are new beginnings and new meanings for me in paths, labyrinths, and mandalas. The direction of my life was changing. Would I arrive at this new life with strength and humor? Would I be safe? Would I be lonely in the future? I tried to find acceptance, wisdom, and something positive in the face of horrendous loss. The mandala is a continuum. It is the circle of life and death. It includes beginnings and endings, and they are indistinguishable. I have wrestled with frustration, anger, and fear. I have cried oceans of tears. I did not want to lose Mark. I could not believe he had to suffer.

When Mark could no longer speak, I told him that it was enough for him to be there to listen. That we were living the simple circle of the mandala. I assured Mark he would continue to express himself and that our family would know his feelings. I told him we would use the DynaVox more often. Or, if we needed to, we would learn sign language to communicate.

"I know the first sign I'm using," Mark said. He lifted his hands and gave the "finger" with both middle fingers. I laughed. Mark's mandala. His circle was full of laughter and full of love. I wondered what my circle would be once Mark was gone.

---

6   Carl Jung, *Memories, Dreams, Reflections* (New York: Pantheon Books, 1963).

CHAPTER THIRTY-EIGHT

Our Children

AS MARK'S VOICE WEAKENED, he worried about not being able to communicate to the children and wondered who they would go to for advice. He felt guilty for leaving and causing pain to his family. He said: "I've always been responsible; this is the flakiest thing I've ever done."

Mark spoke with resignation about being "just a witness." He felt like he was on another planet when he observed conversations in the same room with him but couldn't participate.

I told him his presence was still meaningful. His smile, while looking into their eyes, was intimate. Our children's lives are rich with new experiences, new people, jobs, co-workers, travel, and babies, I told him. Let's just listen and let them share. That's communication and intimacy. It's not intimacy as we once knew it, but it is powerful to be totally there for someone else: no comments, jokes, advice, or anecdotes of your own.

One evening, Jeremy came over and sat on the bed with Mark. He needed Mark's opinion. Mark was voiceless on that day. Jeremy said,

"Dad, you'd probably answer by saying . . . I guess I would respond by saying . . ." The conversation went for almost twenty minutes, Jeremy speaking both parts. Mark didn't break his concentration looking into Jeremy's eyes. Jeremy got up and was satisfied.

Later that evening, Mark painstakingly typed an email to Jeremy with all his thoughts and comments regarding the conversation. This was another pivot. Mark could learn the new steps to stay connected.

One morning, Mark awoke and instantly texted all five children. He asked them to come to the house. The children arrived at different times over the course of the day. I sat in the room as Mark, just above a whisper, spoke with each of them. He told them how much he loved them and how much he enjoyed his life. He said his happiness in life came from being a father. They gave his life meaning and joy. He wanted to exit right.

He said he didn't want them to see his suffering. He hated MSA but wasn't struggling with thoughts of "Why me?" He was at peace with dying. There were tears and embraces as each private conversation unfolded. He made sure they each knew he had experienced as full a life as someone could possibly have at the age of fifty-seven. It was deeply sad for me to sit there and hear Mark say his goodbyes to our children one by one. Our grief can't be compartmentalized. And grief can't be conquered. My grief includes my children's grief.

By the fall of 2013, we were days away from our first grandchild being born, while at the same time, Mark was moving every day closer to death. It felt odd to have these two milestones so near to each other. As a family, we were preparing to celebrate a beautiful new life while at the same time getting ready to say goodbye to another. Finding balance brings gravity. Our family was learning the hard way to, as Francis Weller wrote, carry grief in one hand and gratitude in the other.[7]

---

7   Francis Weller, *The Wild Edge of Sorrow: Rituals of Renewal and the Sacred Work of Grief* (Berkeley, California: North Atlantic Books, 2015).

Bruises

After Mark is gone
I'll repair
the bruises that
streak our home

His wheelchair bumps
along walls
smashing door frames
leaving ripped paint
like scars
everywhere

New gashes made daily
raw
fresh cuts
jagged and sharp

After Mark is gone
I'll heal our home

Seal the damage and
gaping holes
calm rough edges

Like wrapping a wound
with cotton bandages
the sores will be covered
with satin paint
and serene colors

Once I leave
will I return
to wander rooms
and look down
the long corridor?

Will I remember
the bruises
tears
and old wounds
along walls
like lightning bolts
or scars from
a crow's claw?

CHAPTER THIRTY-NINE

Lightening the Load

INSIDE OUR HOME, THE most important task was to get rid of any assistive equipment Mark no longer used. As Mark's disease progressed, and the cane, walker, push wheelchair, scooter, power wheelchair, and other smaller items were of no use, out they went! They were not only bulky and cluttering up our house; these items were reminders of Mark's most recent loss. It was a mirage, but Mark seemed less ill with fewer contraptions in our personal space.

During this time, I made a quick decision to cut my hair quite short. For me, cutting my hair was symbolic of being in transition. I've cut my hair very short a few times before: When I was twenty, I moved to Paris to study art. As soon as I arrived, I found a hairdresser and impulsively cut off twelve inches of my long hair. After we sold our house in LA and were getting ready to drive across the country and move to Raleigh, I cut my hair the day before the journey. It's my way of letting go, leaving something behind, and moving forward.

CHAPTER FORTY

Opposite of Drowning

AS SOON AS I would feel myself emerge from sleep in the morning, I'd keep my eyes shut a bit longer and make a wish. I wished that I would see Mark next to me in bed healthy. We would laugh and say, "Glad that's over!" That's what I was hoping for—a sudden cure, an overnight miracle, all impossible. I looked at a photo of Mark when he was healthy. That was the other Mark, the old Mark. A different Mark. I had to take a moment to remember the way I related to him then.

Just as there are physical plateaus during illness, there are emotional plateaus as well. Traveling from hope to resignation was difficult for me. The few moments I took each morning to make the slow move from sleep to wakefulness helped me find my bearings. I needed time to linger and dream.

I wanted to remain openhearted to the life happening around Mark and me. Pushed by his disease to handle more than I ever thought I was capable of handling, new parts of myself merged and emerged every day.

Two divergent worlds developed: the world with Mark in our home, filled with simple activities like watching movies, talking, and visiting with family and friends; and the world away from Mark when I was by myself, outside our home. It was like living a double life. One night, I went to an event at the North Carolina Museum of Art with friends. There was dancing and food. I knew it would be good for me to get out and dance. Emily, who was working the event, kept an eye on me, making sure I was okay. Initially, having this life away felt like a betrayal of Mark. I would return home and he would always greet me with happiness. I could not imagine returning home and not having him waiting for me.

CHAPTER FORTY-ONE

Remembered Light

SHORTLY AFTER THE INITIAL diagnosis, back in the fall of 2011, Mark announced that MSA would not define him or our family. I understood his meaning at the time, though I had no idea what lay ahead for us. Two years into our journey, I realized MSA had, indeed, defined Mark and our family, but in a different way than either of us could have imagined. I had to align myself with our life situation and accept the grief, struggle, and loss we were living through, as well as what was to come. Tragedy does ultimately break you in pieces. Then, it redirects your life, stretching you in new ways. I had to focus my mind on the things I could do rather than those things I could not. I couldn't provide the medical care he needed. Instead, I reached for rituals of love.

After the CNA left one evening, I got into bed next to Mark and chatted about the lovely baby showers that had been given for Jeremy and Jenn. I told him about the beautiful decorations, darling touches, tiny onesies hanging on a clothesline, and a watermelon carved into a baby carriage. I described the delicious food and desserts as well as laughter in the room as

Jeremy and Jenn opened their gifts. While I spoke, I realized I was calming Mark and myself at the same time. I was giving us both a little bit of peace and a lot of love. We eventually fell asleep hand in hand.

A month later, our first grandson, Noah Mark Freifeld, entered the world at eight in the morning on September 20, 2013. By this time, Emily was nearing the end of her first trimester of her first pregnancy. Our family was growing. Life would go on.

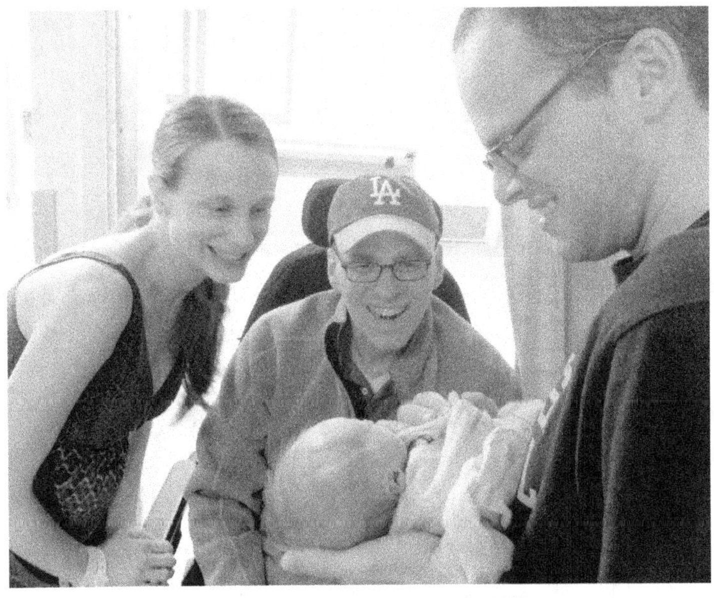

Jenn, Mark, Jeremy, and Noah, 2013.

Afterlife, After Life

I ASKED MARK TO send me a sign "from the other side." He believed once he died, it's over. That's it. Kaput. If he would just send a message, I continued, I would be on the lookout. Maybe, I told him, he'll be the one surprised and say, "What do you know—I have wings!"

I began asking friends who had lost loved ones if they communicated with their deceased family members. To my surprise, I heard all kinds of stories from intelligent people who said they continue to feel someone's presence in different ways. They hear voices, taps on shoulders, guardian angels; they see images in mirrors and receive mysterious calls on cell phones. I heard stories about husbands and wives, fathers and mothers appearing in the guise of hummingbirds and butterflies.

A friend spoke of communicating with her dead mother. Her mother had died more than fifteen years earlier, and since then, they've gotten along much better! Her mother became more empathic to her feelings. I asked her how the communication happens. She answered: "Your inner guide and sense lead you."

My ramblings and questions about the hereafter, ghosts, and messengers from the other side hopefully weren't signs of me becoming a desperate woman—desperate not to lose my connection to Mark after he was gone. Rather, I was willing to ask the unexplainable and, often, the unmentionable. In truth, I hoped I wouldn't go bananas and start talking about Mark sitting in a tree or appearing in the shape of a cloud. I'm imaginative, and I wondered if my strong imagination, added with deep yearnings and love for Mark, could create a communication with him once he departed. This wishful, some call it magical, thinking gave me a sense of comfort.

My cousin, Suzi, said we are to other realities as ants are to people. Ants are going about their daily tasks and working within a social structure. They don't know what humans are doing; ants haven't a clue about the human world around them. Humans, she believes, cannot possibly conceive what is around them. Perhaps there is another reality far beyond what we can see, understand, or explain.

When I spoke with Mark about this, he looked deep into my eyes and said: "I'll be there at the bus stop when you get off."

CHAPTER FORTY-THREE

Eiffel Tower

OUR FAMILY IS A whole. Mark is part of that whole. Mark's disease is an assault on the wholeness of our family. This journey together felt like wandering in the wilderness and taking a journey down a darkened path. Every day was another day in the unknown. We couldn't find a place to rest. There was no familiar face, gesture, or word. Each moment was new, foreign, borderless, and unkempt. There was always a sense of foreboding, uncertainty, and crisis.

Mark and I learned we cannot fix the worries our children have. It occurred to us that perhaps our children needed someone to speak to who is familiar with end-of-life issues. I sent this email to our children. Mark and I had benefited enormously from the counsel of the hospice nurse, chaplain, and social worker.

Hello Everyone,
I was wondering if any of you would be interested in meeting with the staff from Hospice: the chaplain, nurse, or social worker. We can meet and talk as a group, individually, or in any combination.

You've all been on my mind, and I was thinking you might need someone to talk to. Dad and I have been fortunate to speak regularly with these women. We have had meaningful and helpful conversations. Our many questions have been answered, and we have not felt isolated with concerns during the last six months Hospice has been in our life on a weekly and biweekly basis.

I asked the chaplain today, and she confirmed anything can be arranged, and Dad's "team" is available to anyone in our family.

Feel free to ask and say anything,

Love, Mom

After my email, Jenn made an appointment with the chaplain and wanted Mark and me to stay during her meeting. Jenn had many questions and concerns. She wanted to know how to help Jeremy. She wondered what the effect of Mark's passing would be on their newborn son, Noah.

In one month, I thought, she's already thinking like a mother.

The four of us spoke for almost two hours, and it was rich and beautiful. As the conversation neared the end, the chaplain said: "Noah knows Mark, and Mark already knows Noah. They're connected and will always be."

Toward the end of our conversation, Noah became a bit fussy. Jenn, a dancer, got up with her son in her arms and began spinning slowly and moving gracefully, raising her son up and down in a lovely and loving dance.

The chaplain next met with David. David talked mostly about transitions: from college to job, relationships with women that have ended, his journey on the Camino de Santiago in Spain, and just a lot about beginnings and endings.

He talked about traveling through Europe by himself and arriving in Paris and how excited he was seeing the Eiffel Tower. He walked to it the first day he arrived there. On subsequent days, he didn't pay as much attention to the Eiffel Tower as he had on that first day. He simply accepted it as "part of the environment." So quickly, something so great and important to him received nothing more than passing glances. As he caught the train out of Paris, he realized he could not recall which of these glances was his last. Once he left Paris, he realized he didn't know when he'd see the Eiffel Tower again.

When I heard him tell this story, I realized it was an allegory about how David was feeling about his father. And how we take things for granted that they are always going to be there, never thinking about this time being the last time you will see something or someone.

Of course, David connected this meaning to his dad and MSA. He wondered about his dad's "lasts." When was the last time his dad ran, walked unassisted, or drove? When will he speak his last word? When will David have his last conversation and laugh with his dad? When will he see him for the last time? An Eiffel Tower Moment is now the term David and I use when something precious has occurred that we realize we may never see again.

CHAPTER FORTY-FOUR

Mark's Choices

I ASKED MARK WHAT he thinks about these days. He answered (it was a day when he could speak): "I feel contemplative and miss my old self and 'us.' I feel vulnerable because I can't do anything without the help of someone. I feel loved because so many people—you, the children, friends, and helpers—surround me. Yet I feel isolated, frustrated, and sad. The caregivers are taking care of what is left of me. I don't need my body because it is failing. I feel disconnected and isolated since I cannot speak with people when they are in the room with me. MSA is a perfect disease for a wallflower.

"You're only as good as the last thing you did. I don't want to experience every bit of MSA and be remembered that way.

"I cope by not thinking about tomorrow. I may not be here. When I die, you can know I'm no longer suffering. What kind of life is this? My goals are to be comfortable. I'm uncomfortable most of the time. I look forward to seeing my memoir published and hearing you read your book to me. I think about Noah and Emily's baby. They are people who will not know me.

"I've lived with MSA a long time. I don't want to be bedridden for years or have our home turn into an ICU. That is the reason I'm deciding against a feeding tube.

"Our children are not going to make this decision. I want them to understand my wishes and future. They will feel less guilt and anxiety about having done all they could do for me.

"If the time can be predicted, I'd like our children to come over if my death seems near. I've said everything I needed to say to you, our children, my brother and mother."

I went to my computer and pulled up the first fifty pages of my book and read him a few chapters. He stopped me. His face was solemn, and he spoke clearly.

"Actually, I don't need to hear it. I'm living it," he said, but added, "Finish it, because it's important to you."

I closed my computer, and then Mark spoke about donating his brain to MSA research at Mayo Clinic. We agreed it was eerie to talk about, even though we're both organ donors on our driver's licenses. It was creepy for Mark to think about being buried in the ground. Like Alzheimer's, MSA can be definitively diagnosed only with an autopsy. Mark asked if I would want to know unequivocally that he had MSA. I answered yes. I wanted to know what the hell he went through. And by donating his brain to research, maybe we could help rid the world of this awful disease.

CHAPTER FORTY-FIVE

Conversations

MARK WAS AS REAL and down-to-earth as anyone can be. Nothing was difficult for him to talk about. Nothing was off-limits. If Mark and I were having a serious conversation, it didn't end until he made sure we had both said everything we needed to say. I always felt heard and understood. I believe he felt that too.

Mark's ability to look at life's problems directly continued with the way he discussed every angle of MSA and dying. He asked the hospice nurse if he would be aware of when he was dying. Would he hear his family speaking to him if he were lying unconscious? Would she be there at the end? Would he feel pain? Will he remain at home or be taken to hospice? What's easiest for Julia, he wondered. I wanted to hear the answers, too, while simultaneously wanting to grab my hat and head for the hills. I was aware, but Mark was more aware. He found knowledge comforting. I did and I didn't.

After a particularly bad day, Mark asked the nurse if he would be alive tomorrow. He was unable to get out of bed and could barely speak. He had an infection and felt the way a healthy person might feel if they were slammed with a hundred pneumonias all at once.

I was in the room with Mark and the nurse.

"Mark," I said, "You're having a dip, you'll spring back after a few more days of antibiotics."

He turned his gaze toward me. The nurse did too. He laughed and stammered. "As my mother would say, 'I just need to lay low.'"

The three of us laughed.

Mark's mother, Doe, often overstates the obvious and understates the most serious moments. Her husband battled emphysema, a serious heart condition, and various other ailments for years. Through it all, she was his primary caregiver. Since his death, she'll often remark, throwing her hands in the air, "Out of the blue, Danny died."

Soon after Danny's passing, she moved to Raleigh to be near us. One day, she asked me if Mark had been to see a neurologist, adding, "This came from out of the blue, yet gradual." This is her coping skill. She is both in denial and aware at the same time. I now understand my mother-in-law better than I have ever understood her before, and I believe she is right about one thing: a little denial goes a long way.

The social worker told Mark that when he neared the end, he would be able to let go of his life and say: "I'm ready." She told me people who are dying are able to know when to say their final goodbyes and that our family would reach a point where we would want Mark to be released from his suffering.

I could not imagine.

It seemed unfathomable. "Letting go" sounded like a stupid cliché. I didn't know what the hell it meant.

CHAPTER FORTY-SIX

Normal/Strange

I LOOKED OUT MY window and became mesmerized by the trees. A few months earlier, they had been covered with green leaves. The leaves did a shimmy, and one by one they broke off and were released from their branches and fell to earth. The limbs were now bare. The seasons were flying by in a snap.

By the first week of November 2013, I began my menu planning and pulled out the Thanksgiving decorations. I was sitting next to Mark, upstairs, by his chair, and he said: "Today is my last day." Each day, for almost a month, Mark repeated those words to me.

Once, after Mark announced his notion that this would be his last day, I went to our dining room and pulled out a drawer full of linen tablecloths. Was the rich brown or autumn yellow best for my table this year? Should I add bits of pineapple or diced oranges to my cranberry relish? Again, a little denial goes a long way.

I'm not a hermit or a martyr, and I believe in pleasurable moments each day. Besides preparing for a beautiful Thanksgiving dinner with our children, I was social with friends, going to the gym, and playing with our new grandson, Noah, for whom I had just finished a hand-painted wooden highchair.

But Mark was suffering. He wasn't in a lot of physical pain. His pain was emotional. Mark assumed his death would take ten steps; instead, it was ten thousand. There were little deaths, small losses each day. Those losses accumulated. Each month, Mark had to sacrifice more privacy, freedom of movement, and speech than he had imagined possible. We kept thinking he was hitting the bottom each day, yet there was still far to go. As he continued to decline, his failing health and independence required the CNAs to do more for him. This need for help was as huge and debilitating as the disease itself.

One night, Mark was getting ready for bed with the assistance of the CNA, a process that could take over an hour. All five children and Noah were hanging out with me in the family room while the CNA worked with Mark. David turned on some music and we all danced, having fun imitating one another's dance moves and taking turns dancing with Noah. Although taking a moment to dance and laugh might seem strange under the circumstances, it was far better than hovering by the closed bedroom door.

A whole lot of normal pressed up against a whole lot of strangeness.

A few weeks later, Emily had an early morning obstetrician appointment. I arranged to be with her so I could hear her baby's heartbeat. My neighbor said she would stay with Mark until the CNA arrived.

My morning routine began earlier than usual. I rushed to get dressed and give Mark his medicines, which he now had to have crushed and mixed with applesauce. As I brought the spoon to Mark lips, he turned his head away. He did it once more. I broke out in a sweat, and my eyes filled with tears. I didn't understand what was happening.

Was he suddenly refusing his medicine?

Mark couldn't speak. I blurted, "Are you refusing your medicine? Do I need to call the nurse? This would be an emergency, and I have to hear Emily's baby's heartbeat today!"

I saw a small smile emerge at the corner of Mark's lips. Clearly, I had missed or overlooked something.

Mark used his finger to point to the bed. I hadn't raised the head of his bed. Mark was lying flat, and he was refusing his meds because he would have choked taking them lying down. I quickly found the remote control device and raised his bed, and he took his medicine.

We laughed at the absurdity. There were multitudes of absurdities.

CHAPTER FORTY-SEVEN

Attending a Wedding

IN EARLY DECEMBER, I accepted an invitation to a friend's daughter's wedding in New Jersey. Emily was going with me. If Mark's health changed, I was prepared to cancel up to the very last moment. I had learned to say yes to everything until the moment I had to say no. Mark and I nicknamed ourselves "the Undependables" because we were regularly canceling our social engagements at the last minute.

To say I was amazed when I got to the gate with Emily at the airport would be an understatement. I was flabbergasted. It had been seven months since I last left Raleigh to go to the beach with my book club. When the plane took off in the early morning, I calmed down and was glad to be on my way. We landed in Newark and made our way to the hotel.

Emily and I decided to visit New York that afternoon. We thought we would go sightseeing, have a meal or two together, rendezvous with a friend of Emily's, and see my cousin who lives in the city. Traveling to New York from Newark by train looked easy on the map. Just a hop, skip, and a jump, right? Wrong!

We spent a ridiculous amount of time, about two hours each way on the train, going to and from New York. This could have been stressful, but we managed to laugh about our mistake. I found the enormous crowds of people everywhere a mix of soothing and entertaining. I felt like I was walking through a Diane Arbus photograph. It was a great distraction.

We ran hand in hand down one of New York's gigantic boulevards in search of a restaurant in SoHo I had heard about. We ate hamburgers, then ran almost all the way back to Penn Station laughing more, because it was impossible to get a taxi. Finally, just a few blocks from the train station, a taxi stopped for us. We had no time to see anything else or visit with anybody. It ended up being a four-hour trip for two hamburgers!

The wedding took place the next day. From our lobby-facing balcony, Emily and I ate breakfast and watched the bride and groom being photographed below. We viewed the rows of chairs being set up and the elaborate chiffon-covered *chuppah* (wedding canopy) as it was constructed. The activity below captivated both of us and made us feel tranquil.

Around three o'clock, we joined the other guests on the main floor of the hotel. The festivities were a whirlwind, with a beautiful ceremony and a high-energy celebration afterward. Following the wedding, Emily and I changed into comfy clothes, joined a gathering of fellow Raleighites in a cozy section of the lobby, and chatted for several hours.

A week or so later, I received two handwritten letters from two guests at the wedding. They arrived a few days apart. Both were written on cream-colored stationery in blue ink. Neither person knew the other had written to me. However, each carried a similar message.

They each said how glad they were that Emily and I could come to the wedding and enjoy the time away. They talked about not knowing what to say to comfort us about Mark's illness or how to help. The letters were warm and heartfelt and took me by surprise.

The impact of these two tender letters was profound. I carried them in my purse for weeks. I reread them and reached out to both women with gratitude. I know that if I have a friend going through a similar thing, I will write to say something. It was the most thoughtful thing either one of them could have done for me.

CHAPTER FORTY-EIGHT

Another Year

WITH WISTFUL SMILES, MARK and I clinked glasses. There were no toasts or words. It was midnight, January 1, 2014.

Mark was alive. We had made it to this season. We didn't reminisce about 2013 nor discuss the year ahead since we had no travel plans, weddings, or graduations in our family. Our second grandson was due in April. I felt certain Mark would meet him.

February rolled around, and I felt steady. I didn't question my mood. Relief. My bright yellow forsythia was about to bloom, adding brightness after a long winter-gray landscape.

I stayed afloat and kept an eye on our children, making sure they were staying afloat too. We were all bobbing along.

The previous fall had been harder. Maybe it was because Mark was certain he was going to die any day. By winter, he no longer expressed that opinion.

During the night I occasionally watched Mark sleep. He smiled and talked out loud, sometimes making a high-pitched sound. His eyes fluttered rapidly. He was not in distress. I wondered if his dream life was more free and pleasurable than his waking life. I wondered if he was walking, or running a triathlon in his dream. I gently laid my hand on his wrist. He opened his eyes and focused on mine, and we smiled.

Mark hadn't been on the first floor of our home since Thanksgiving 2013. He stayed upstairs in our family room or bedroom. The children came by on Saturday evenings. As soon as Jeremy and Jenn arrived with baby Noah, Jeremy would dash upstairs, placing Noah on Mark's lap. We'd all be there: Jeremy, Jenn, Noah, Emily, James, David, and my mother-in-law, Doe. The news or sports on TV would quietly play in the background as some of the children sat on the couch with laptops open. There was a pleasant banter, and people casually getting up to do this or that.

We sat close. We celebrated the birthdays and anniversaries as they moseyed on by. We played games. Sometimes Jeremy, James, and David got out their musical instruments and played. We all sang to Noah.

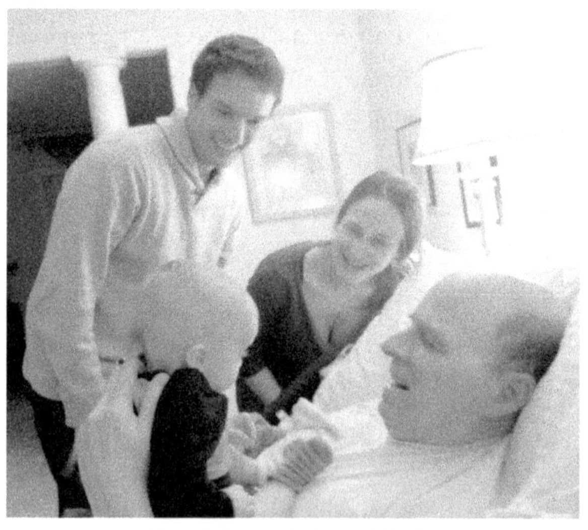

David, Jenn, Noah, and Mark.

Sometimes we'd all climb into bed with Mark and watch a TV show or video clips of one thing or another. Often David took a moment to arrange the pillows. While he was doing this, he'd take an extra moment to lay his head on Mark's chest, close his eyes, and hug him.

Emily, seven months pregnant, with Mark.

The most fun was plopping Noah on the pillow next to Mark and laughing. I snapped photos with my cell phone of it all. I snapped pictures of the wheelchair, scooter, and medicines piled up on the bedside table. This was our milieu. These items were the background of our lives now.

I didn't plan on taking photos of Mark at this point. But our moments together were precious. I hoped to capture the transitory moments we were living. Like an impressionist painter, I hoped my photos would capture the light.

Decisions

I ARRIVED AN HOUR early to hear two journalists speak at a local independent bookstore. Since my hearing is bad, I prefer sitting in the front row. I always arrive early to be able to claim my seat. Emily and James were going to meet me. When I arrived, a handful of early birds were already there.

I stood in front of all the rows of white plastic chairs and surveyed my options. James is tall, so I knew he'd likely prefer an end seat or one in the back. Emily is shorter, so if she sat with him, she might not see as well. In my mind, I debated the pros and cons of different arrangements, placing my sweaters on various seats, changing my mind, and selecting two other spots. A woman was next to where I planned to sit and was watching me carefully.

When I sat down beside her, she turned to me and looked directly in my eyes and said, "You're a person who makes a lot of decisions in life. You were careful making the right one just now."

"Yes," I answered. "I'm constantly making decisions."

She was a writer and said she was inspired to write a "flash fiction" piece on me.

I wonder if it ever got written.

CHAPTER FIFTY

Upstairs/Downstairs

DEBBIE (JAMES'S MOM), JENN, and I hosted Emily and James's baby shower at our house. It was an intimate gathering on our first floor. The three of us decorated the house the afternoon before and put up the final touches the day of the party.

I was hoping Mark would rally the strength to join us downstairs by the time the gifts were to be opened. It was clear on the day of the shower that Mark was weaker than he'd ever been. He remained upstairs. I remained downstairs the entire party and had a fabulous time. I was not feeling torn that I should be with Mark rather than celebrating Emily's baby. I was all smiles and felt the joy of the evening.

After the party I lay beside Mark in bed. Emily joined us too. Mark said he was in no shape to have been at the party. He wasn't complaining or angry. He wanted to hear every detail and see all the gifts. He wanted to know that Emily had had a magnificent time.

I was living in two places: my "upstairs" reality and my "downstairs" reality. I wondered the next day how I could compartmentalize so completely.

Our second grandson, Max Chandler Kotecki, entered the world at 2:14 p.m. on February 9, 2014, eight weeks early. No one in James's family or ours had had a preemie. He was meant to be with us early so Mark would have more time with him. Mark was determined to go to the hospital to see Max. It took one of our CNAs and Jeremy to get him there. It was the last time Mark left the house.

In May, I made the decision to go to dinner with our family and Jenn's family to celebrate Mother's Day. Mark was at home with the CNA. I felt happy being with the children, our grandchildren, and extended family.

Toward the end of the meal, I got up to go to the restroom. When I returned the waiter was standing at our table (smiles all around, and all eyes on me) and asked if I was Julia. I told him yes and noticed he was holding a piece of cake with a candle in it.

"This is from Mark," he said, "to wish you a happy Mother's Day."

I burst into tears. Someone helped me to my chair. My careful emotional compartments had fallen apart.

Mark holding Max in the NICU with Emily and James, February 2014.

CHAPTER FIFTY-ONE

March Magic

THERE WAS NOTHING ANYONE could do to keep Mark from dying. MSA, which is filled with the unknowable, has no clearly defined ways to move through its slow, determined progression from life to death. We had no way of guessing what was going to happen or how long Mark would be with us. We kept steady even though we were grieving a living person. Yet our grief wasn't a straightforward Kubler-Ross model of five stages of grief: denial, anger, bargaining, depression, and acceptance. With Mark, there was no order. By March 2014, he was living longer than expected. I could go through all these emotional stages in an hour, backward and forward. If you're a naturally reflective person, you'll have a field day during the grief process.

Mark wondered if he'd do a "Stephen Hawking" and live past the usual trajectory of MSA. Mark had been rethinking his life and possibilities. For several mornings, following difficult nights, he typed on his iPad: "I'm still fucking here, UNBELIEVABLE."

We were coasting now, no predictions in sight, no more "This is my last day."

Mark had basically no strength left. He could barely type an email. So we got a Hoyer lift. The Hoyer lift is a large metal frame on wheels with a sling attached. To move Mark from his bed to the wheelchair or reclining chair in the bonus room, the CNA would put Mark in the sling. He looked so helpless. This is when I saw his sadness. Even though he always held his chin high when he was rolled down the hallway, we didn't want the kids or anyone to see him in it. One of our goals was to protect and preserve his dignity, and this contraption amplified his weakness.

One evening, Mark was participating in a webinar with other MSA patients. The online support group offers tips, resources, and camaraderie. Mark's speech became softer and slurred, and at times he would stammer. After everyone on the webinar introduced themselves, Mark quipped, "I can hear we all have the same accent." There was no response. Mark looked at me, winked, and mouthed the words: "Tough crowd tonight."

More March magic: after a month in the neonatal intensive care unit, Max was home and thriving. He would at last be joining us on Saturdays, in the thick of things with our family, placed near Mark on a cushion, enjoying music and laughter.

The same week Max was born, Mark's memoir, *Reflections*, was published. It was selling on Amazon, and we were excited when we heard from readers. Mark's book touched people through his humor, wisdom, and coping capabilities. I reminded Mark that his book would be placed on my bedside table and remain there the rest of my life.

Surprises came in abundance in March. Mark was astounded when one of his favorite journalists, Fareed Zakaria, sent him a copy of his book along with a personal note. Emily knew somebody who knew somebody who knew Zakaria and had the book signed and sent to Mark. Mark wrote him a thank-you email, including information about MSA and other rare diseases. Lo and behold, in the middle of March, Mark received another book along with a personal note from Zakaria. This time his gift came without a nudge from anyone. We were over the moon! Mark happily wrote another thank-you note and included *Reflections* as a gift to Zakaria. One good turn deserves another.

Mark had reached many benchmarks and milestones in the last year. He witnessed Jeremy and David's graduations and saw them start their first jobs. After David graduated, he decided to live with us. After work or weekends, he stayed near Mark, arm in arm. They often looked into each other's eyes and smiled. Mark celebrated with Jeremy when he passed the bar exam. He finished his book. He met and held both grandsons.

Could surrounding Mark with oodles of love, laughter, goals, and family slow down the progression of MSA? Could the instability of MSA be balanced with rituals of love and kindness?

All I know is, there was a lot for Mark to be here for.

"I didn't know I had so much to do," Mark said, smiling.

CHAPTER FIFTY-TWO

Freak Out!

I WOKE UP ONE morning, stood at the end of our bed, and made it perfectly clear to Mark that he could not die in his sleep! No can do! It will FREAK ME OUT, I told him. I repeated: It will freak me out, freeeeek meeee owwwt! FREAK me OUT!!! You may have different ideas, but "I Will Freak Out. I will freak out. I will Freak Out! I will freeeek OUT!!! I WILL freak out!!!!"

I couldn't stop repeating this. I said it almost fifteen times, each with a different emphasis: fast, slow, one part of a word drawn out, loud, and then whispery. Mark was lying in bed laughing as my hands swung in circles, arches, and straight lines with pointing fingers to emphasize the words. I made imaginary exclamation points and periods in the air. My eyes darted around the room. I smiled, laughed, and made all kinds of animated faces as it occurred to me just how freaked out I would be if I woke up one morning and found Mark had died and was lying next to me.

Later that day, I received an email from Mark:

"As far as dying in my sleep, no guarantee. I'll try not to freak you out, but do you want me to pass peacefully? 25% of MSA patients die in their sleep . . . Or, if at bedside with family, then I want a mariachi or klezmer band at bedside unless you find the idea annoying and silly/goofy. I'll remind you we signed a no willful guilt no willful freak out *ketubah*[8] . . . A rarity in Jewish marriages. I already violated the no wedding and recarpet house in the same year clause."

Humor is powerful. It bonded Mark and me. If Mark had reacted defensively or angrily, my reaction would have been different. I might have moved away emotionally from Mark. His humor kept me near.

Mark did not let go of me. He was tied to me; therefore, he was tied to life. Mark and I were on a teeter-totter; when one of us was down, the other was up, but not for long. We managed to stay in balance by watching each other and making each other laugh. Sometimes, however, it felt like the seven of us in our family were on a seven-way teeter-totter, keeping an eye on one another, making sure no one fell off.

Several days later, I told my worry about Mark dying in his sleep to the hospice chaplain, who described several other possibilities:

Mark does die in his sleep, and you don't freak out. You wake up and notice he's died. He may be cold or warm depending how recently he passed away. The color in his face may have changed; he may be gray.

You gently take his hand, and it may be a spiritual moment for you. You feel his presence or you don't. You talk to him or reflect on memories.

Now I knew there were many possible ways to react. I felt relieved. She continued, raising her hands and moving them in synchrony:

---

8   A ketubah is Jewish wedding contract.

Julia, you've reacted in an organic way throughout Mark's long illness. You and Mark have remained together, harmoniously. You've adapted and made changes when needed.

I absorbed her every word.

CHAPTER FIFTY-THREE

Widow-World

WE NEED MENTORS THROUGHOUT the chapters of our lives. We also need our peers. By observing and learning from healthy examples, we gain understanding of how to be a friend, spouse, parent, grandparent, widow, whatever our life stage.

I had lived in my subdivision more than seventeen years and never gone to our neighborhood Ladies Club before. The lecturer sounded interesting, so I went. It was in a home I'd never been in before, but once inside, I recognized a handful of friendly faces.

As I poured a cup of coffee, a woman approached me with a smile. She had heard through the neighborhood grapevine that my husband was on hospice care. Her husband had been on hospice care before he died. Now, there's an icebreaker!

We found each other after the meeting ended and resumed talking as we made our way to the door. We were just about to head to our cars when another woman appeared and joined the conversation. She asked when my husband died.

"Not yet," I answered with a surprised chuckle.

Her husband had died eight years earlier. She was pointed in her questions: Are the bills in both our names? I mentioned I had just gotten a credit card in my own name to begin establishing my own credit. Good idea, they both agreed. We decided the three of us would meet for lunch the following week.

I had just found my new peer group.

We made a lunch date. I brought a small notepad and pen along to take notes. They spoke openly, advising me to write the obituary, make the funeral programs, and select the music for the funeral service ahead of time.

As I was leaving, I recognized another widow walking through the restaurant. Now, when I see a widow, I find myself staring. Time slows. I become riveted. I imagine their lives with their spouses and without them.

River

Like a river I meander into
the tiniest of streams where you can't see me
I flow beneath the surface
underneath the ground
finding the bottom

If you're standing on a riverbank
I'm beneath you
hiding
finding the flow
avoiding the murky
unmoving swamp

Like a river, I gather nutrients
by changing my course
it's done so slowly
no one can see it happening

Rivers meander
that is how they restore themselves
cut rocks
move boulders
carve away all that is in their path

CHAPTER FIFTY-FOUR

Details

AS THE END NEARED, Mark's breathing worsened. He felt pain and needed morphine for the first time. Jeremy administered it orally with a medicine dropper. I needed to get organized; that's the message I was hearing from friends and our hospice team. It felt like bad luck to do certain things ahead of time, as if taking action could cause something to happen to Mark.

I took another walk in the neighborhood to clear my mind and move my body. I felt completely alone. I walked every curvy street and tiny cul-de-sac. Solitude is necessary during difficult decision-making. The children were arriving the next day, and it was time to have a heart-to-heart meeting with them about the next phase of our lives and how to prepare.

Doe, Jeremy, Jenn, Emily, and David arrived as planned. James was out of town on business. There was the natural flow of chatting and playing with babies. After lunch, the children and I were cleaning up in the kitchen, the perfect moment to initiate our discussion. Mark was upstairs sitting in his chair. His mother was keeping him company.

I started the conversation. I wanted them to know that if their dad died in his sleep, or if he died without warning, I was considering contacting them by sending a text to all five of them simultaneously. It would simply read: 911. They nodded and said that would be fine. We decided that when Mark died, we would call hospice, and they would alert the funeral home. Mark would be taken from our home, and we would never see him again. There is no open casket at a Jewish funeral.

I asked how they thought we should announce the news of Dad's passing. Which of the children should make the calls? Should we call by phone? Use email? Facebook? I showed them my mishmash list of phone numbers and email addresses. The children had their own lists of friends to call and tell. David mentioned he had his email ready. I was surprised.

We all decided I should have one email ready to send, as well. David put it together while we continued the conversation. Jeremy offered to call Mark's brother, Richard; my sister, Caren; and all the grandparents.

Together we decided Facebook and email were acceptable ways to communicate someone's death. It isn't crass or cold as I worried it might seem. It's acceptable these days. I asked who would feel comfortable writing the obituary ahead of time. Emily offered to do this part.

I told them about the plans that had already been made for the funeral. Everything had been arranged. Dad's friend Jonathan would be in charge. The funeral would take place at Temple Beth Or, and the two rabbis would conduct the service. Three people would give eulogies. There was no pressure, but they were welcome to speak. Jeremy immediately nodded, indicating his plans to give a eulogy. The burial would follow the service in a cemetery in Chapel Hill. We decided that if there were more than three people who wanted to speak, they could speak during one of the nights of shiva in our home.

After our conversation, I felt unburdened. We had discussed and delegated all the necessary arrangements. My children continued to amaze me. We pulled together, helping each other during this unusual and amazing journey. We were making our way together to the end.

CHAPTER FIFTY-FIVE

A Turning

MY CELL RANG AT six thirty in the morning. It was our neighbor worried something had happened to Mark. On her way to work, she noticed fire trucks and police cars parked in front of our house, with lights flashing.

I was in bed. I turned to Mark, who was lying next to me, and asked if he was okay. A wobbly arm was raised and a thumbs-up given.

I told her all was well here.

I ran downstairs and headed outside. It was pouring rain; there had been storms throughout the night. I discovered lightning had struck our next-door neighbor's house, and the firefighters and police were checking on the family's safety.

Even though it felt like lightning had struck our family, this time we had missed an actual thunderbolt.

Yet recently something had hit me—something surprising and sad.

I had to uncouple, though nothing could break my heart more. Usually, the grief work and uncoupling happens after the death. I needed to start when he was alive. I was pulling away and preparing for a life without Mark. I had to let go of feeling safe and protected, being touched and caressed, having conversations, and sharing experiences both outside and inside our home.

Once Mark was no longer able to eat solid foods, I ate my meals alone in the kitchen before joining him for the evening. When we no longer shared meals and couldn't have our usual discussions, the "us-ness" of our relationship altered. Mark saw it happening before I did. He wrote in his book, *Reflections*:

To Julia: one of my greatest pains is the loss of my relationship with you. How do I process this? I don't focus on the sadness and pain simply because I can't. These feelings are always there, but I choose not to let them gain control. I can only focus on the years we spent together, the laughter, the sheer joy, the family we created, and the overall experience of our life together. Every time I came home I came into love, your smiling face and warm hugs. It was exceptional and I am truly grateful. It could not have been better.

I am thankful to have had the opportunity to love you. I just wish I had more time. I think no matter the timing, I would always want more. I never want it to end. My love is deep and flows through my veins. For me, I've been living the ultimate life experience, and the experience we shared was full . . .

I cherish the life we have shared. I love you forever.

When Mark and I married, we were both twenty-six years old. We ritualized our joining as husband and wife under the chuppah, which was open on all sides to allow the community to be part of our lives. We said words of commitment. Our family and friends sang songs to envelop us in love. In this ceremony we became coupled. I made a promise to Mark: "Till death do us part." I would not abandon him.

Yet we were uncoupling. Or maybe I was unraveling. I felt alone. There were many layers of letting go of a life. First on the outside, as Mark's outer life, such as work, dissolved; then on the inside, as the disease progressed. Our us-ness was dissolving further. I felt the space between us enlarge; an emptiness took over.

A Mirage

I stand by the window
Looking through two types of glass
Plate glass offers the clear view

Crackle glass
animates the outside world
A slender branch fragments
Rustling leaves kaleidoscope

I close one eye
images liquefy
An ordinary red brick
moves like water
The sky ripples
Rooftops look like brush marks
Colors blur like watered silk

The crackles are like threads
looping their delicate way
around the glass

The interlaced facets
are within
the soft pane

PART
IV

SUMMER 2014:
MARK'S DEATH

Laugh

MARK COULD NO LONGER speak, but he was mouthing a word. He typed two letters, LA. That was all the strength he had. I guessed the word, "laugh." He nodded almost imperceptibly. He thought I was getting too serious and reminded me to laugh.

Perhaps we should try to get out of the house, have an outing, maybe see a movie, I optimistically suggested. It was almost impossible to get Mark dressed and down the stairs. I was willing to if he wanted.

He moved his lips, shaping the words so I would understand: "There isn't a movie I need to see *that* bad."

I took a two-hour class on music used to comfort those at the end of their life. It was another eye-opening moment. I approached the teacher and told her about Mark. She was a volunteer for hospice, and I was able to arrange for her to meet Mark a week later.

She brought a variety of wooden flutes and singing bowls. She spoke with Mark and me a few minutes before she began playing the instruments. She improvised, responding to Mark's breathing. The singing bowl was placed near Mark's head. The type of music she created was free-form and less rhythmic. There was no pulse or discernible beat. She defined her mission as healing the body, mind, and spirit through the vibrations of sound. She saw her music as a bridge between the earth and the heavens, and hoped to ease a person's physical pain, emotional fears, and anxiety.

Mark didn't seem that moved. I forgot to reread his email about having a mariachi or klezmer band brought to his bedside. He might have enjoyed one of those more than flutes.

CHAPTER FIFTY-SEVEN

July 4

I ALWAYS REFERRED TO MSA as a storm that entered our lives. July 1 was a pivotal day. While the nurse examined Mark, listening to his lungs, taking his temperature and other vitals, a huge storm began gathering outside. First, it was just a drizzle; soon thunder and lightning surrounded our home. Mark had a high temperature. The nurse said he had pneumonia.

I was living moment to moment. It was difficult to eat and drink. How much information did my children need to know? They had their daily lives: jobs, spouses, small babies to care for. My life was by Mark's side. It could be claustrophobic for all of us to sit together every minute in a small room where Mark was lying. Ultimately, I told them Dad's health had worsened. They had made it clear to us from the start that they wanted to be notified of changes in his condition.

But Mark remained full of surprises. The next day he had a bit of a bounce up and decided he wanted a gathering of our friends on the Fourth of July. It was also our anniversary. But we didn't mention that to anyone. Mark wanted to see people, perhaps say goodbye in his own way.

I sprang into action. I figured out my menu: cheese platters, fruit, and cupcakes in a pattern of the American flag! I made a blue margarita punch. I let friends know to come over between four and six. It was going to be a celebration. The kids and I discussed whether we should allow one or two people upstairs at a time to see Dad. There were logistic issues, like who should be with him and helping to communicate for him, since he couldn't always speak.

The CNA got Mark dressed in a white polo underneath a sunny yellow sweater, and gray sweatpants and shoes. He sat by the window in our upstairs bonus room. Almost forty people arrived within minutes of four o'clock. There was no way to limit the number of people to be with Mark. They all headed upstairs and surrounded him. Mark smiled and had a twinkle in his eye the entire time.

Mark wanted one friend to meet another since they both had kids at NYU. Other friends were introduced because Mark remembered they both had knee replacements. Mark communicated with a slight nod while looking at a particular person, then the other person. People eventually figured out the connection on their own.

Although they knew it was probably their last time to see Mark, everyone was eating, drinking, talking, and laughing. It didn't feel like death was imminent. It wasn't teary, scary, or sad. We often had Fourth of July parties; this felt like just another one of them.

DREAM: Mark's funeral had begun before I arrived.

CHAPTER FIFTY-EIGHT

Prior

TEN DAYS AFTER THE party, Mark developed pneumonia again. Mark pressed the nurse, wanting to know how long he had left. She said under a week. All the kids rushed over with their suitcases and babies. Doe arrived too. We gathered in the bonus room around Mark, and I explained the situation.

Doe's head sank to her chest then rose, "Do you mean one week?" Her head sank again then rose. "Seven days?"

"Yes," were our answers to both her questions.

Each of us said another goodbye to Mark privately. I told Mark I loved him, and I would miss him terribly. I'd manage somehow without him and would think of him every day.

It was time. We were ready to let him go. We were prepared for the next transition, Mark's passing. His suffering and ours would end soon. Later that day, I called other family members. Mark asked me to update friends via email. The kids sent emails to their friends, co-workers, bosses. The next day, Mark rested. He did not open his eyes.

On Thursday, July 17, Emily's birthday, he opened his eyes and looked around. His breathing sounded normal, no longer gurgly. The pneumonia had subsided—a miraculous recovery. Mark assumed he would be in the 20 percent of MSA patients who died suddenly. It began to appear that he was maybe in the 80 percent, the ones who lingered.

Jeremy came by with Noah a day after Mark's recovery. Mark wanted to wear one of his specialty T-shirts, the "Fuck This Shit" one. Jeremy and I each wore one too. Even Noah had one on.

Mark began eating and drinking again, even asking for a beer. His hope, by eating and drinking, was to aspirate and develop pneumonia again.[9] He was seeking a way out. However, he remained steady for four more days.

I wondered if Mark had pressed Beth, the RN, too hard. Was it a good thing to know how many days? Was she right? I had been on a death watch for three years at that point. Mark's final days with MSA were as awful and rocky as ever, with starts and stops, plunges and recoveries.

David said he felt like a rag doll, picked up by the collar, thrown against one wall, then another. He described the 2011 David vs. the 2014 David. In 2011, he was not emotionally prepared for the MSA diagnosis. Three years later, in 2014, he was prepared for Mark's passing.

When Mark recovered from pneumonia a second time, James admitted to feeling angry. "Mark's suffering was going to be prolonged as well as all of our suffering. I didn't really want to go in that room anymore. I didn't know what to say. I had a couple good conversations with him right after the first pneumonia. I had another conversation with him after that. And then another conversation I was kind of awkward, like, I was trying to talk about politics, and thinking, does he even want to hear about this? I didn't know how to be in that room anymore."

---

9   To "aspirate" means to inhale food or drink into the lungs.

The tension was thick. I felt we all needed air. We didn't know when the end would be. And, as James said, "We couldn't hang around by a thread, circling around his bedside every moment of the day. We have to keep doing stuff that's what he would have wanted us to do."

Since Mark had improved, I made a quick decision. Emily and James had a family reunion to attend in the DC area. They weren't sure whether they should leave town. I called and told Emily to go, get out of town for a couple days and do something normal. They went.

David and I needed a break too. I suggested we spend half a day in Pinehurst, an hour away. The CNAs would take care of Mark while we were gone. Jeremy and Jenn moved in to help, so we were fine to leave.

So, right in the midst of the most excruciating week, David and I took a long drive out of the city. We found a lunch spot and then returned home. Our playing hooky from caregiving duties for the day can be forgiven, I hope.

By the time David and I arrived home, Mark had made a decision. He wanted to stop eating and drinking. It was illegal in North Carolina to take your own life via medication. So, he did what he could control, and that was to simply stop food and water. I never considered he would do this. But I agreed with Mark's decision. He didn't want to leave us, but he didn't want to go on.

I don't think Mark or our family had an opinion before MSA about the right-to-die movement. We have strong opinions now.

The hospice social worker had once said, "You will reach a point where you'll want him to be released from his suffering." I was horrified and angry at her suggestion. In retrospect, she was right. His suffering needed to end, as well as our family's suffering.

James added, "It's this whole emotional roller coaster. He's going to die very soon, actually, nope, now he's getting better, and he could live for however long. Now, he's not eating or drinking. How long can a human being live without food or water? Is he still getting water? Is someone sneaking him some food or water? Is that going to prolong the process even more? I didn't want to think about it too much. It was this roller coaster. I couldn't get on a timetable anymore. I told some people at my office, 'Hey, I might be out this week, my father-in-law is going to die.' Then he gets better, I felt like I was bringing other people along on this ride, too, that I didn't want to bring along."

Mark was not in physical pain because of the morphine. I rubbed ice chips along his lips. I sat by his side. That was the beginning of his last week.

On that Monday, Emily and I decided to have a Shabbat dinner and her birthday celebration on Friday, the twenty-fifth. Just the kids, grandsons, Mark, and me.

On Wednesday, the twenty-third, Richard called. He and his wife, Sarah, wanted to fly in. We discussed several possible dates. He planned to arrive Sunday, the twenty-seventh. The next day he called and had changed his mind. They would arrive Saturday, July 26, at six in the evening. Fine with me.

CHAPTER FIFTY-NINE

On the Day You Died

THE BOOK *On the Day You Were Born* by Debra Frasier tells the sweet story of the birth of a child.

While you waited in darkness, tiny knees curled to chin, the Earth and her creatures with the Sun and the Moon all moved in their places, each ready to greet you the very first moment of the very first day you arrived. On the day you were born . . . you slipped out of the dark quiet where suddenly you could hear . . . a circle of people singing with voices familiar and clear . . . "Welcome to the spinning world, we are so glad you've come."[10]

Saturday, July 26, 2014, was an ordinary and extraordinary day. Looking back, it was perfect. It was sacred. The planets and stars were in place. The heavens were awaiting Mark.

The sights, sounds, smells are still fresh in my mind. In the same way parents remember a child's birth, all the details are there. It is a moment on the edge, a threshold. It is holy and intimate. There is a birth canal to life and a death canal to somewhere else.

It was a day and night that took us by surprise. We each had our own experience.

---

10   Debra Frasier, *On the Day You Were Born* (Boston: Houghton Mifflin Harcourt, 2012).

Mark's usual morning aide wasn't there; neither was his nurse of sixteen months. Both were off that weekend. A young aide we'd never met showed up around eight. Her job was to get Mark up, dressed, and ready for the day. She entered the bedroom, closing the door behind her. I waited outside the room. When she came out of the room, she walked into the hallway looking worried.

"How is he this morning?" I asked.

She wouldn't answer. She said she needed to contact the nurse on charge that day. She said she wasn't allowed to say anything.

I pressed her: "What do you mean? What did you notice?"

"The color of his lips, nails, and fingers," she let slip as she stood by my front door. She said she was going to contact the nurse and ask her to come by that day. I could tell she didn't want to say more, and I didn't press any more. I watched her walk down the brick path to her car.

I called my friend, a retired neurologist, and asked her to come by. She arrived in fifteen minutes. She examined his skin, suctioned him,[11] looked into his eyes. As she was about to leave the room, she told Mark, "I love you. I'll miss you. Let us know what you find on the other side."

When she came downstairs, she told me he could live a few days or more, or even just a few more hours. It was hard for her or anyone to say.

The hospice nurse on call that day arrived a few hours later. We had only met this nurse once before. As per her instructions, we continued the morphine that hospice prescribed to keep Mark pain-free and relaxed.

The rhythm of the day was calm, slow, and natural, the front door opening and closing, people flowing in and out of our house.

Jeremy, Jenn, and Noah came to the house around three thirty. I hadn't expected them to come. At the last minute, they decided to spend the night. It surprised me. Around four thirty, Emily, James, and

---

11 "Suctioning" is the process of removing mucus from the throat.

Max arrived as planned months earlier. They were celebrating Emily's birthday together, dropping off Max on their way to dinner and a dance performance in Durham.

By this point, meals were being dropped off daily. My friend Leni brought over a roast chicken around five. Leni and I had a casual and lovely visit on my red chenille couch. She and I took turns holding Max. Perhaps thirty minutes later, Max fell asleep sitting up on Leni's lap. Another twenty minutes or so went by; Leni handed Max to me and left. Minutes later, another friend, Tracy, arrived to lend a hand babysitting Max.

David was staying in that night, Skyping with his Spanish girlfriend, Lucia.

THIS IS WHAT TRACY REMEMBERS:

I remember letting myself in without knocking. I wasn't sure where anyone might be and didn't want to disturb what could be going on. I found Julia sitting on the red couch holding Max. He was quiet and still, peaceful in her arms. I could tell by Julia's posture and how still she was holding Max this was a sacred moment. It was like the stillness captured in a painting. Very still. Julia whispered hello to me. I sat next to the two of them. We didn't talk. The room was getting dark as Jeremy came in swinging ten-month-old Noah in a Moses basket. Noah was giggling.

Julia asked Jeremy to go to the pharmacy to pick up a prescription for morphine. He left. Jenn came into the room. Noah was still in the Moses basket on the floor. The three of us were smiling at him. Noah smiled back.

Julia said, "I have to go upstairs and see Mark. Can you watch Max?" She handed Max to me. I didn't see Julia again that night. I knew her place was by Mark's side, and she would not be joining us the rest of the evening.

Max became fussy; Jenn suggested he was hungry and brought me his bottle. David stepped into the room; we said hello to one another. Jeremy returned from the pharmacy and took the medication upstairs. When he returned to the kitchen, he suggested the rest of us should eat dinner. I wasn't hungry but joined them at the kitchen table. Max was nearby in his baby seat. Jeremy and Jenn sat next to each other eating the roasted chicken and feeding Noah. The conversation was light, mainly about work. We were all dancing on the surface, Jenn and Jeremy choosing not to betray their worries. It was a beautiful family moment.

After forty-five minutes or so, Jenn said it was time to get the babies ready for bed. I didn't want to impose, but Jenn asked if I would like to bathe Max and put him to bed. She invited me to be part of their family. We went upstairs. Jenn got the water running (it had been a long time since I bathed a baby). Max was enjoying his bath. I bundled him in a towel and went into the blue bedroom. I laid him on the white comforter and gave him a new diaper and dressed him in his clean pajamas. I closed the door once Max became fussy. I knew Mark and Julia were in the bedroom near us, with the door closed and the crack of light at the bottom of the door.

It was around eight, and I was by myself with Max. He started to cry. I knew Mark and Julia were right there and didn't want to worry them. I started singing the Barney song, "I love you, you love me," and "Lullaby and Goodnight."

Max calmed down and fell asleep in my arms. He was in my arms when the door swung open. It was Julia. I softly said, "Julia." She didn't say anything. She closed the door. I saw the pain in her face. I knew.

I placed Max in his little bed. After he fell asleep, I walked downstairs and stood in the kitchen by myself. The house was totally quiet and totally dark except for one floor lamp near me.

I was alone in the kitchen. I heard the clock ticking. Five minutes passed. I couldn't just leave without telling someone Max was okay. I was there to help with Max; his was the life I was responsible for.

I heard footsteps running down a hallway above me. I heard Julia wail. Then silence.

I heard someone running down the front steps. It was Jeremy. He was composed, but I could feel a deep sadness in him. I said, "Jeremy. I'm so sorry." We hugged in a way that expressed our great loss, his and mine too. I was crying; I felt comforted by him. He said, "Thank you for being here." He didn't say anything about his dad, just . . . he knew I knew. I said, "Give your mom my love." Jeremy went right back upstairs.

I let myself out, got in the car. It was 8:45 p.m. I started sobbing and didn't stop till I got home where my daughter and husband waited for me.

THIS IS EMILY'S STORY:

I was there Friday. Dad had changed since I last saw him a couple days earlier. I was seeing him dimming. His expression was more frozen. His eyes were looking at me and at a distance. He had a faraway look.

He didn't smile.

I told him about work; he nodded. I placed Max next to his hands on the bed. I couldn't stay more than five minutes before returning to my old bedroom to cry. This is different, he's not there.

I left Max with Mom and picked up Grandma Doe; she stayed an hour with Dad. After her brief visit, I drove her back to her apartment. Grandma Doe told me she couldn't be with him too long; she didn't want him to see her cry.

I kept trying to make Dad comfortable. I suctioned him.

I was watching someone die.

The nurse Beth came by that afternoon. I left their room; it was Mom, Dad, and Beth. I remember pumping my milk for Max in my room. At some point Jenn, Jeremy, and Noah arrived. I was thinking, when will James be here? When I heard James pull into the driveway, I ran to him and burst into tears. My dad looks awful, I told James. James held me.

We were all there to celebrate my birthday and Shabbat with the family. I thought, let's bring the candles upstairs by Dad's bed.

We were all there, in a circle, around Dad's hospital bed. I remember holding hands. Lila, the CNA, stood behind us. She came around and hugged each of us before slipping out of the room and leaving the house.

I lit the candles; we recited the prayer without crying. Jenn was next to me, James on the other side of me. Dad looked deeply at each of us. We were silent. Our faces glowed by the candlelight.

Jeremy, Jenn, Noah, David, Max, and James headed downstairs to the kitchen. Mom and I were the last to leave the bedroom. Mom asked Dad if he'd like to listen to music, perhaps the Beatles?

He kept pointing to his iPad. He tried opening it. He repeatedly made a tent with his hands, fingertips touching, palms slightly spread, almost in a clapping manner. He couldn't but seemed desperate to speak and communicate what he wanted. We could not figure out what he wanted to tell us. Dad closed his eyes; the music played. When we saw he was comfortable, Mom and I went downstairs to join the others.[12]

We sat at the kitchen table. Jeremy took off his glasses, put his head in his hand. Jenn leaned over him. We were all crying. Jeremy raised his face and said, "Boy, I'm really going to miss Lila." Wow, did that break the tension! We laughed and ate dinner.

Before I left to go home that night, I went back to see Dad. I said, "I love you, goodbye." I cried really hard all the way home.

The next morning, James asked if I had had any dreams last night. He said he dreamt Dad died. I said I did too.

Saturday afternoon, I met David for lunch and shopped at REI, I was getting items I needed for the triathlon a couple weeks later. I asked David

---

12   Several years later, in thinking about the night before Mark died, I remembered him tenting his hands over and over in frustration trying to tell us something. It was only then that I understood what he was trying to say. He was trying to tell us we needed to stay together. Which we have.

what is the code if I need to come home immediately? Mom's is 911. David's was "Time to come home."

That night, James and I were going on our first date night since Max was born. We had made plans a while ago. Mom's friend Tracy was going to be there to help Mom babysit Max.

We arrived around four or four thirty, I explained Max's schedule to Mom. I peeked in on Dad; he was sleeping. We took a few photos in front of our house with Max on our way out. We went to dinner in Durham at Watts Grocery (I kept checking my phone), then headed to the Reynolds Theater for a three-act dance performance starting at seven thirty. We saw the first act (I had turned off my phone). At the first intermission, I turned it back on. No messages. At the end of intermission, as we sat back into our seats, and the lights in the theater were dimming, I checked my phone again. At that moment (8:42 p.m.) a text appeared from David: "Emily, time to come home." I showed it to James. It felt like we were jumping stairs. I typed "coming" (8:43 p.m.). When we were outside the theater, I called David.

"Is he gone?" I asked.

"Yes," David said. He was crying.

"Don't move him before we get there," I told him.

"We won't."

James was driving and focused on getting us home safely. He was holding my hand. He looked in shock.

"I don't have a dad anymore," I said.

I ran in the house and up the stairs, into Dad's room, I saw Dad and fell on the floor. I knew it was real. Mom helped me up. I gave Dad a hug, my head on his shoulder.

Uncle Richard, Aunt Sarah, and Grandma Doe appeared soon after. I stayed with Dad and Mom, then left the room. Mom said, "Before the funeral home arrives, say your private goodbye now. It will be the last time you see him." I went in alone, and then James came in. I told him I'm going to miss him, miss talking with him, sharing things with him. I know he wasn't suffering anymore. I gave him another hug and held his hands. I removed his wedding ring. When James came in, he really started crying.

Later that night, James went to sleep. Jenn was with Noah. I stayed with my mom and my brothers. Around one in the morning, I saw Dad being taken down the stairs covered in a sheet, under a cloth of darkness. I was thinking this would be the last time I was going to see him. This would be the last time he'd go down the stairs. I'm never going to see him again.

Jeremy, David, and I were downstairs. We said goodbye to the nurse as she left our home. Then the three of us hugged by the front door.

JAMES'S LAST TIME SEEING MARK WAS FRIDAY EVENING WHILE WE LIT THE CANDLES AROUND HIS BED. THE NEXT DAY, SATURDAY, WAS HIS DATE NIGHT WITH EMILY. HE RECALLS:

Before we headed out, someone took a picture of me, Emily, and then Julia photobombed it with Max. I remember looking at that and posting it on Instagram and thinking: This is a very weird juxtaposition, a very happy moment, and the people in it are very happy, but also they're not. I just remember thinking that was an odd picture.

We had a fun night out, actually. It was Emily's birthday celebration. We had a great dinner, then went to the dance festival. It was the most incredible dance performance. I was floored by it. It was amazing scenery, lighting, and dancing. They were all gyrating in a weird way like amoebas. It was incredible, and that was just the first act. I was excited to see the second two acts. Between the first and second act, obviously, is when we got the text.

We ran out. I didn't want Emily to drive. I went into emergency mode. I had to be focused and get Emily home. Emily was starting to cry in the car, and I don't think I was as much. I focused on driving; I knew I had to get there safely.

Julia, Max, James, and Emily, July 26, 2014.

I remember telling Emily, "I don't know what's going to be waiting for us when we get to the house, but I had a really good night with you." I didn't want to lose the memory of that, or the fact, for those few hours, we had a really nice time together.

A lesson I learned from this experience, from the way Mark and Julia set the tone for the rest of the family, is it's a given you can have these joyful moments. Mark and Julia chose that as an attitude from the very beginning. They set that as an example and established that over and over again throughout Mark's illness, and that is basically why we went out that night. We did know he was going to die very soon. If it had been another scenario or another family we might not have gone, but we felt like we could, and I'm glad we did.

We came home. It was quiet. We ran up the front stairs. Emily fell on the floor when she saw Mark. I was very sad.

I remember going in and out of the room a couple times, and each time his color got more and more white. I had never seen someone right after they died, I was surprised at how quickly the color changed and went out of his face.

When everyone went in to speak one last time, I went in with Emily and told him, "Sorry my last conversation was pretty awkward. I didn't know what to say. You were a great father-in-law."

I loved him. It was very sad.

THIS IS WHAT JEREMY REMEMBERS:

I remember going with David on Friday to pick up two loaves of challah from Whole Foods. And, when Emily proposed bringing candles and lighting them around Dad. At first, I wasn't sure I wanted to do that. It was like: "Oh, we're about to go and do something really emotional now. I was imagining it being a very heavy moment, I was anxious about that."

After we lit the candles, Dad was not moving much, but I remember him looking at us, and looking satisfied in some way. I'm glad we did that. That's a nice memory, and it's good to do something meaningful. Dad always liked Shabbat, so that was meaningful for that reason.

We came over the next day (Saturday) at around three thirty. I brought Noah up and saw Dad. I remember his eyes were open. I held Noah. Dad could see us. He was looking at us. He was conscious and could see us. He looked especially weak, weaker than I had seen him before. The time went by, and I went in at another point to check on him, around four; his eyes were closed.

At around the same time, the nurse showed up. She didn't stay long.

Later in the evening, Mom asked me to call hospice and order oxygen. They called me back and said, "We're on our way, we'll be there in twenty minutes." The phone call came ten minutes after Dad died. At that point I said, "Oh. You can cancel it. Cancel the order."

Shortly before Dad died, I remember checking his pulse and timing his breathing. The breaths were one minute apart.

I went to get David. Maybe ten minutes had gone by. When we came in, actually, it looked like he wasn't breathing at all. We checked his pulse, and he wasn't breathing. I got Jenn. She was in the bonus room with Noah. Max was sleeping in Emily's room, where Tracy had put him down. I went downstairs; I saw Tracy. I remember she was crying and hugging her. I don't think anyone told her, but she got the sense of something. She left the house right afterward.

The next thirty minutes was just walking back and forth down the hall, into the room, talking on cell phones, calling hospice, calling Uncle Richard, calling the nurse, the funeral home, lots of phone calls.

Each of us had a moment alone with Dad. David was first. Emily, James, me, Jenn, and last was Mom.

I felt there wasn't just one goodbye. There were many moments, I didn't have a definitive goodbye moment. I had said goodbye in different ways, multiple times over time. It was an ongoing conversation. I had said everything.

HERE'S JENN'S MEMORY:

I remember Tracy coming over and taking care of the babies together. I have a clear memory of bathing Noah and Max and trying to do everything according to Emily's instructions.

I remember being in the bonus room when Jeremy came in to tell me his dad died. I don't remember his exact words; it was matter-of-fact, and he was remarkably calm and focused on getting things done. It was a shift, like, "Okay, I'm the patriarch of the family, it's official." He stepped into that role.

I looked into Jeremy's eyes, hugged him, and asked, "What can I do? How can I be most helpful? That's my role tonight."

It was an interesting back-and-forth for me. Giving myself a little time to grieve but wanting to be supportive. It would be selfish to just focus on myself, but I had to make sure I gave myself time to experience all my feelings too.

I remember coming into the room and not wanting to look at the bed where Mark was. I just focused on Julia.

Julia asked if I wanted to see him. I looked at Mark. My reaction was: Oh, that's not Mark. It doesn't feel like Mark anymore. His face was so white. A little later, and it may have been my imagination, he felt like he was glowing. Maybe he's still in there! I don't know, it sounds ridiculous and funny.

I remember Julia wanted to sit and just look at Mark, take him in, savor his presence. That was really remarkable; it was a lot to take in.

I remember Julia saying, "Jenn, I'm going to need help making decisions. Will you help me?" I held her hand and said, "Okay, we'll make decisions." But Julia made great decisions right away about the day and time of the funeral, when would be best for traveling family and friends.

I remember our private final goodbyes, before the men from the funeral home arrived who were going to take Mark downstairs and out of the house. I realized this was the last physical form of Mark I was going to see and the last chance to say something to his form here. I wanted to talk to him. Mark was so generous and accepting. I felt so accepted in his presence. Even his little blinks, he brought so much presence, love, and generosity. I've always been amazed at this. He was so consistent and amazing, even in his last moments; it was beautiful. He was beautiful.

I think Jeremy felt a little funny talking out loud to him, which I understood.

I remember David curled up and sobbing after his last time alone with Mark. I tried comforting him and wishing Lucia were there. I couldn't be the one who comforts him the way he needed to be comforted.

I'm so grateful for Mark sharing his readiness to go. It made it significantly easier to tell Mark, once he had made the decision not to eat or drink: Okay, if this is what you want, I'm all in and supportive. I want you to know that we release you, I release you. Not that I had that power to release, but I'm not holding on in any way. I know this is what you want. I want that for you.

I remember touching Mark's feet earlier in the week before he died, I don't remember which day, it might have been Friday. The blankets were over his

*feet. I remember rubbing Mark's feet and trying to put Noah down on the bed.
I wondered what it was like for Noah, what was Noah perceiving?*

*I remember Mark wanted to see if Noah could walk. Jeremy and I tried to
get Noah to walk. As you know, he's still not walking.* [laughs]

DAVID DESCRIBED HIS DAD'S FACE AS HAVING A VERY NICE CALMNESS ABOUT IT, A PEACE WITHIN IT. BUT AS HE DESCRIBED MARK'S LAST WEEK, THERE WAS A NOTICEABLE SHIFT:

*In the face of illness, Dad was selfless. He was able to look at you, pay atten-
tion, and be there. When you have a week left to live, you're pretty much forced
to be lost in your own mind. He felt there, looking into my eyes, but felt sort
of mentally next-step.*

*Previously, he could find humor in anything, find these kind of little
joys. But, that final week, he really wasn't much for jokes. I sensed a mental
difference. He wasn't trying to put any kind of soft cushion on anything
anymore. His mind was in this final stage. He had put up a defense
around himself to enable other people to feel comfortable. That protection
was down, and I can only imagine, just sort of trapped in his own mind,
reflecting on his life. It was a raw week. His physical state was in total
decline. He refused antibiotics, food, and drink. He had pneumonia and
knew what was coming.*

*I had to convey, in a series of conversations, whatever would allow Dad not
to worry about us. To let him know how strong I felt our family had become.
How much we'll miss him and how much we loved him. Anything I could do
to help him and to let him know we'll be okay.*

*I would have wanted him there until I'm eighty or ninety years old. I don't
think there's a typical age to lose a parent, and given a healthy relationship, I
can only imagine that somebody will want their parents until they themselves
are a hundred years old.*

It was the final week. We were only there to say real things. It was a very, very, very profound week. It didn't call for lightness or distractions.

Friday night during the candle lighting, I felt very in-tune and intimate with everyone. Dad was sort of back to his peaceful and loving expression. I emailed Lucia to let her know the situation. I wrote that night, pressed send, then went to bed.

On Saturday I asked Mom if it would be okay to take Dad's photo.

I walked in, took the photo, and walked right out. I knew he'd hear the click; it's loud. He would think, "What are you doing?" I noticed his eyes fluttered a bit. I realized he would understand.

In the afternoon I went for a run. I met Emily for lunch and joined her shopping for some things she needed for the upcoming triathlon. We talked about having a code we could use to let Emily know to come home immediately.

When Jeremy, Jenn, and Noah came over, I got out my camera again and shot some photos of Jeremy throwing Noah high in the air. I took a shower, lounged around, and Skyped with Lucia. She booked a flight to come out Wednesday. I read a little and texted with Lucia.

Jeremy came into my room; he wanted me to come to Mom's room. Mom had noticed something different about Dad's breathing. When Jeremy and I entered, Dad had already passed away.

The last time I saw Dad alive was sometime between noon and 2 p.m. At that point he was breathing heavily, leaning to the left, eyes closed. I held his hand, asking him if he could hear me. He gave a very, very subtle response of "yeah." Maybe it was a blink, or a movement of an eyebrow. I told him I loved him. I said that a few times. I kissed his hand and walked out.

When Jeremy entered the room that night, we checked vital signs but didn't feel a pulse or feel breath coming from his mouth. He felt cool. Mom was sitting next to him, holding his hand, and started crying very hard.

Immediately, Jeremy and I went into business mode. I texted Emily using the code we had decided upon: "Time to come home."

Jeremy and Noah, July 26, 2014.

I was in the room with Dad when Emily and James walked in. I remember seeing Emily collapse, which was really hard to see.

I remember the nurse arriving around ten. She stepped in, we stepped out. She put Dad in a more comfortable position. She pulled the sheets up, placed his hands together, and made him look peaceful. Uncle Richard, Aunt Sarah, and Grandma Doe arrived and sat with Dad too.

It was necessary to have our private time with Dad. I talked to him and cried. I already told him what I wanted to say when he was alive. I just looked at him, like taking a photograph with my eyes, trying to remember that final image of him. I took in the room, the look of everything around him. I kissed him on his forehead and walked out.

Jeremy, Emily, Mom, and I sat at the top of the staircase and watched the funeral guys take Dad out of the house on a stretcher.

I was talking on the phone with people from Duke University Hospital, Mayo Clinic, and Jonathan regarding the brain donation. I got called three or four times through the night. About every hour and a half someone else called.

I helped Jonathan organize the Hava Nagila [laughs] or whatever it's called. [Chevra Kadisha][13]

I woke up Lucia and told her what happened and what I wanted. She said, "Okay, David, all right." We were both emotional. She reminded me she'll figure out the flight stuff and will be there Monday. But, for the time being, she reminded me to be with Jeremy, Emily, and my mom. She kept saying, "Be with them," she loved me, she will be there soon.

MY MEMORY:

I remember the house was full of people. Jeremy, Jenn, and Noah arrived Saturday afternoon around three thirty, and for some reason it surprised me. Soon after, Emily, James, and Max came by. Leni and I visited briefly in my family room after she dropped dinner over. Max was with us. Minutes after she left, Tracy appeared. I remember handing Max to Tracy after she arrived around six and saying, "Can you watch Max? I have got to go upstairs and be with Mark."

I walked up the stairs and entered our room. Mark was alone in the hospital bed in our sitting area. The room was dimly lit. His eyes were closed. I sat in a chair to his right and took his hand. He was facing to the left. I didn't take my eyes off his face.

I was relaxed knowing Jeremy, Jenn, Noah, and David were in the house. I knew Tracy was taking care of Max. And Emily and James weren't far away, having a nice evening out.

---

13   Chevra Kadisha is a volunteer organization of men and women in the Jewish community "who see to it that the bodies of deceased Jews are prepared for burial according to tradition" and are with the body until burial.

I had no sense of how much time had elapsed. I had never watched someone pass away. I didn't understand what the different types of breathing are or what they meant. I didn't think he was dying that night.

When his breathing changed, I thought he was struggling for oxygen. His breathing became heavy, loud, and labored. I called Jeremy to come in. I asked him to listen. We both agreed it was labored. He's struggling for oxygen, I thought, and asked if Jeremy could call hospice and order some oxygen to be sent over. Jeremy said yes.

By the time Jeremy returned, Mark's breathing had changed again. It had gotten slow. Jeremy timed it with his phone. A full minute would pass before he took another breath. We timed it a few times. Jeremy checked Mark's pulse in his neck. Jeremy left to get David.

I was alone with Mark. I was holding his hand. He took a breath and, at the same time, his chin pressed into his neck, and his head turned toward me, which seemed like a monumental feat. I glanced at his fingers that were draped over mine. They became white; then purple swirls like watercolor appeared.

I was alone with Mark when he died, which was amazing because many people were in the house.

The very moment after Mark passed away, Jeremy and David appeared in the room. David stood by Mark's head, and Jeremy near me. They were checking his vitals. I continued looking at his hand and cried out, "He's gone." And burst into tears.

Jeremy and David had their arms around me, and the three of us hugged.

It seemed as though only minutes had passed before Emily and James appeared. I was by Mark as they entered our room. Emily looked right at Mark; a second later she fell to the floor, crying, her large mass of curls flying. I leaned over and lifted her up. James stood very still behind her. She quickly walked over to Mark and placed her head on his chest; her hair covered Mark. I looked at James; he remained in the exact spot, looking intensely at Mark.

Richard and Sarah's plane landed in Raleigh at 6:30 p.m. Less than thirty minutes after they arrived at Doe's apartment, Jeremy called them to let them know Mark had passed away. It was perfect and uncanny that Richard decided to switch his flight one day earlier. He would not have seen Mark if he and Sarah had flown in the following day as had been originally planned.

The three of them showed up in our room around nine thirty. They surrounded Mark. I remember Sarah putting her hand on Mark's shoulder and speaking directly to him. Doe and Richard each had time with Mark as well. They stayed an hour or so before leaving.

The hospice nurse, who had visited earlier in the afternoon, arrived. She made the official declaration of Mark's passing at 10:00, even though he had died an hour and a half before. She asked us to leave the room while she cleaned Mark and rearranged his body.

It was just the kids and me with Mark. I just couldn't sit there anymore. This strange energy emerged. I had to get rid of the things that were connected with Mark's illness.

I asked Jenn and Emily to help me clear away all the medical stuff from the bedroom and bathroom. We threw everything into huge trash bags. We worked quickly.

When the two funeral guys arrived in the doorway of my bedroom at midnight, I thought it was a joke. One guy appeared to me to be very tall, maybe eight feet nine inches, the other very short, four foot two. It felt comical, surreal, and bizarre. They didn't seem professional. They asked if I had funeral plans. Of course I had arranged plans, a year ago! I was becoming angry. I had barely displayed anger in the three years since Mark's diagnosis or all the years before when he was becoming symptomatic. Quite unexpectedly, all my anger poured out on those two guys.

"Mom, we'll take it from here," Jeremy said. He motioned for me to sit on the bed.

Jenn wondered what made me so angry with them. They seemed nice enough to her. She said to me, "I'm sure they had worse moments with people."

Around one in the morning, the nurse asked me to leave the room, as they were about to transfer Mark from the bed to a gurney, cover him, take him down the stairs and out of the house. She assumed I shouldn't watch.

I went to the bonus room and peeked out the door as Mark, covered with a blanket, was removed from our bedroom. From a distance I saw him taken down the stairs. I walked down the hall near Jeremy, David, and Emily. The four of us sat at the top of the stairway. We quietly watched. Mark was in the foyer. The men stopped, added a white cloth to cover his head, placing the blanket once again over his head. Jeremy's head dropped in his hands for a moment.

Mark on the gurney and the two men were out the door into the dark night.

By two thirty, I was in my bed.

CHAPTER SIXTY

After

I DON'T REMEMBER FALLING asleep or waking up the next day. All the kids and grandkids spent the night; in fact, they spent the week at the house. We all noticed having trouble with our computers the first few days after Mark's passing. We weren't able to connect easily with the internet. It's like our computers were shut off. Eventually, after the first couple days, the devices began working again. I later heard from others that this is common following a death. It has something to do with the energy of the deceased person interfering with the signals as it leaves this world.

The temple made the funeral a turnkey operation. The rabbi came over to speak with all of us. He listened as we shared stories and memories of Mark. He had Mark's book with him, and we selected the parts we wanted him to read at the service. As a family, we chose a three-day shiva. The women from the temple who organize food for the shiva were contacted.

Family and friends from out of town began arriving Sunday and Monday. I was grateful Lucia was with David by Monday. The funeral was noon on Tuesday, July 29.

The outfit I wore had been hanging in my closet for several months.

As planned, the limo arrived at our home to pick up our family. I had assembled a large basket of snacks to bring with us: nuts, fruit, granola bars, and water. James sat in front next to the driver. I was in the middle of the second row, between David and Emily. Lucia, Jeremy, and Jenn were in the back seat as we drove to the temple.

Along with Mark's mother and brother, we met with the head rabbi in a conference room. She handed each of us a black ribbon to wear over our hearts. We tore the ribbon, and a prayer was recited. The torn black ribbon is a symbol, an expression of grief, anger, and brokenheartedness at the loss of a loved one.

We were led toward the sanctuary. It was filled, including the balcony.

I linked arms with David and Lucia. The three of us walked down the aisle. Jeremy and Jenn, Emily and James followed behind us. I saw faces swirling around me along the aisle. Through my tears, I kept my eyes on the simple pine wood casket on the *bimah*.[14]

All seven of us sat in the front row.

Both rabbis were available to lead the service. A young woman from the congregation sang beautifully. There was something in the way she sang that made Jenn feel Mark's presence.

The three eulogies were given by his brother, Richard, our close friend Jonathan, and our son Jeremy. They spoke lovingly and with humor. There was laughter through the tears. Several friends told me later that they were comforted hearing my laugh during the service.

When the service ended, I stood outside the temple. A receiving line formed spontaneously. I remember the hugs and whispered words in my ear: "I love you . . . I love Mark . . . I'm so sorry . . . I'm here for you, your family, whatever you need."

---

14   The *bimah* is the altar in the synagogue.

Soon, we were on our way to the cemetery. I felt my anxiousness grow as we got closer.

James liked the Jewish traditions surrounding the burial of the body at the cemetery. This is how he described the graveside service and the shiva at our home in the days after:

My most vivid detail was the sound of the dirt hitting the casket. It was the most memorable detail of the whole week. If I had to choose one sensory experience, just one second, to explain what it was like, it would be that. When the rabbis took the shovels and when I heard the sound, "poomph," that just destroyed me. I started sobbing and kept sobbing most of that part of the day. I cried a lot while that was happening. All my grief came outward. It needed to come out, you shouldn't repress it.

The car ride to the cemetery and back was nice too. We were sad, we were happy, we were silent, we were laughing. We did all those things because we're not programmed to be in one emotional state the whole time. If Mark were alive and he lost someone, he would be showing all that range of emotions too.

I loved the three nights of shiva. I loved seeing who came and who supported the family. I loved seeing the people we didn't know from the temple helping with food and everything. It was like a Freifeld party: the food was good, the drinks, the brandy Alexanders on the last night. Everybody from the Hanukkah parties was there, and it was just like it always was when the Freifeld friends and family got together.

At the gravesite, during the burial, my cousin Jeannie and others noticed a dragonfly buzzing nearby. They noticed it because it stayed near them for such a long time. In many cultures, the dragonfly symbolizes the soul of the person who has died. Dragonflies can be reminders or spiritual connections to the afterlife.

The first night of shiva was the hardest. My house rapidly filled with close to a hundred people. I felt foggy as I sat on the couch with my children and Doe. The brief service was led by the rabbi. Family and friends stood and told stories about Mark.

I retreated to my bedroom before the crowd left. I heard the rise and fall of voices from downstairs while I hid under my covers.

The rabbi gave me a tall red shiva candle that would burn for seven days. It became a symbol of Mark. I kept it with me day and night while home. Each night I placed it on my bedside table. I'd watch the flickering of the glow of the flame on the ceiling as I fell asleep.

I worried about the day the flame would go out. The day it did was another day of loss. It was the last flicker of Mark's presence.

As I had throughout Mark's illness, I leaned on ritual as a guide and comfort after his passing. I leaned into my community for support. Their presence alleviated some of my anxiety. On Friday night, I went to Shabbat services. I knew Mark's name would be read that evening and would be for four consecutive Friday nights following. That is part of the thirty-day mourning period in Judaism following the burial called *sheloshim*.

I sat near the middle of the sanctuary. Family and friends were on both sides of me. I picked up the program and opened it to the last page where the names of all the people who had died that week were listed. There was Mark's name. I sat completely still as I stared at his name.

The familiar prayers and faces surrounded me. During the singing, I remembered Mark, years ago, sitting next to me during services, his lovely voice blending with the congregation.

Mark's name was said, and the Mourner's Kaddish was recited.[15] I kept my tears from exploding out of me by inhaling and sucking in short bits of air. As soon as services ended, I darted out of the temple and headed home.

I slept deeply. In the middle of the night, I felt someone brush against my hip and then lie on their side facing me. The bed sank in heavily. I felt the weight of a body there. It felt as real as life. I woke up and looked to see who had entered my room and got into bed with me. No one was there. I screamed, cried, and moaned all at the same time. The sound was like nothing I'd ever made before.

I stayed up for almost four hours, tossing and turning in bed. I wondered why bodies are placed in the earth, returning to Mother Earth. What does it mean to bury someone? What are you burying? A memory? Is burial a comfort? I recalled the dirt hitting the casket. "The echo of earth falling on the wooden coffin is the terrible and haunting sound of finality."[16]

I got out of bed and wandered through our home. What were Mark's life, death, and burial supposed to teach me? I realized what I had to learn had not happened yet. My lessons were just beginning. Once I understood that, I returned to my room.

When I fell asleep again, I dreamt I was screaming angrily at several people. Someone left a mess somewhere, and it made me crazy. At the same time, I was trying to take care of my baby. I held my baby. There was so much tension coming out of me while I tried taking care of my baby. He turned whitish-blue, and then I laid him on the floor.

---

15   The Mourner's Kaddish, or Mourner's Prayer, is said in honor of the deceased. This prayer focuses on life, promise, and honor of family and individuals of the Jewish faith. Retrieved from http://www.shiva.com/learning-center/prayers/kaddish/.
16   Anita Diamant, "Filling the Grave: Shoveling Dirt onto the Coffin Is the Family's Final Ritual Act of Honoring the Dead." Retrieved from MyJewishLearning.com.

DREAM: I'm in a car in the driver's seat. A friend is in the passenger seat. My arms can't reach to steer the wheel. The car drives over boulders and through bombed-out cities. I'm not able to control the wheel.

DREAM: Mark and I are walking at a rapid pace, fused shoulder to shoulder. I look down and see Mark is walking. We look at each other. Then he says, "I have to go." He gets into his old brown Volvo and drives away.

CHAPTER SIXTY-ONE

Afterlife

A WEEK AFTER MARK'S passing, I had an appointment with my dermatologist. I was with a nurse I had never met, and I blurted out that my husband had just died.

"He has a new body. You'll see him again," she said with a smile. I found this incredibly comforting!

Jeremy and I were running an errand together. While driving, I told him about my 2:30 a.m. brush with Dad in my bed and a call I received in the middle of the night when all I heard was gibberish. He mentioned a weird phone call he received in the middle of the night from an unfamiliar number soon after the funeral. The voice was male, and the message was odd and incoherent.

A few minutes later, when we were still together in the car, a motorcyclist darted in front of us from the left. His license plate read "afterlife." He was in our lane, directly in front of us for a few minutes. Jeremy craned his neck to get a better look at the leather-clad motorcycle dude. The driver quickly veered into the right lane and exited the freeway.

"Dad?" Jeremy asked as the cyclist disappeared. We looked at each other, smiled, and laughed.

Later that same day, I was driving by myself. A van was in front of me with a license plate "Partyof5." Mark always referred to our family as the Party of Five.

Two nights later, my home phone rang again at 2:30 a.m. I answered; no one was there. What time zone was Mark in? Was I getting messages from license plates? Is there an afterlife? If it helps to believe there is, why not? It's a glass half full idea and still eases my pain.

CHAPTER SIXTY-TWO

Hollow

EMILY AND I WERE at the cemetery one afternoon, and she expressed her worry Max wouldn't know Mark. I said Max will know Mark through the stories we will tell and by sharing our memories of him.

A few nights after visiting the cemetery, we went to hear stories being told at The Monti, a local live storytelling venue. David was one of the storytellers that night. Coincidentally, four of the stories were about fathers. Emily and I kept looking at each other. Two of the stories were about fathers who had passed away. One was given by a woman in her sixties recounting the memory and loss of her father when she was around Emily's age. There she was on stage with tears in her eyes, still missing her father, holding him close through story and memory.

For weeks after Mark's funeral, dying no longer seemed natural. Illness and dying seemed bizarre. I was not prepared to not see Mark again.

It was a new world for me. The world with Mark and the world without him seemed worlds apart. It's like your world before and after having children—incomparable.

I had to let go, release, say goodbye, bury, pray, and cry.

I had trouble sleeping at my home sometimes. It felt hollow. Occasionally, I slept at my neighbors' homes. I needed holding. I could have fallen into someone's arms and been held for days.

Late one night, I sobbed. I realized I didn't know how to check a life insurance deposit online. I was angry at myself for not knowing how to do such a simple thing. I had so many learning curves ahead. I was hesitant to text Jeremy about the deposit. Suddenly, I was remembering Mark's burial, his casket being lowered in the ground. I sobbed more. David was still living at home at the time, and I couldn't decide whether I should wake him and ask for his help with my question.

I texted my lifelong friend Naomi, who lives in California. She called me right away. "At this hour, there is no banking going on, no deposits are being made. You can't open up a new account. You'll learn this stuff. It will take time, that's all. And it's a good idea not to wake up David or text Jeremy." She carefully, bluntly, and with humor brought me down to earth.

More important, she said it's not weird to think about the funeral. She still thinks about her brother's funeral from 2009.

A few days later, I met with my rabbi. I needed direction. She made a bowl with her hands. "Embrace the hollowness and sadness. Don't rush the sad feelings, hold them, feel them, then let them pour out."

"Where is Mark?" I asked. "I don't feel him when I visit the cemetery."

"He won't tap you on the shoulder, but if you're open to the possibility and to the signals, you can experience his soul when you're with others that loved him. You'll feel his presence," she answered. Emily, David, and I felt his presence at the storytelling evening during the many father-centric stories.

The rabbi talked about a tree in front of the temple that had died. "The trunk is hollow, and the branches have been dead a long time. Yet a seed dropped in and is growing inside—new life blossoming inside a dead tree. It's a perfect metaphor of Mark's soul. His personality was too large and too grand to not be springing to life in a new way for us."

Every time I remember Mark, I refresh Mark's life. I kindle the light of his soul.

CHAPTER SIXTY-THREE

Mountain Retreat

SHORTLY AFTER MEETING WITH the rabbi, I drove to the mountains to spend a week at a hotel. I was eager to be alone and anonymous. I could exercise, hike, and spend as much time alone as I needed.

Before leaving that morning, I joined our family to watch David, Emily, and Mike (James's brother) as they crossed the finish line after completing a sprint triathlon in Chapel Hill. It was the same race Mark ran in a few times before MSA, and it has since become a yearly tradition for Emily along with anyone else in the family who wanted to join her.

As Lucia, Debbie, and I waited at the finish line, we spotted a dragonfly circling us. We all pointed and remarked about the dragonfly at the graveside service.

After the triathlon, I got in my car alone. I had tears in my eyes as I waved goodbye to my kids. The three-hour ride to the mountains alone was a peaceful and thoughtful time.

I was going to be alone for seven days. A retreat, a rite of enclosure. Words flowed through my mind as I drove up the mountain: readjust, recalibrate, and redirect versus remain, maintain, and sustain.

I checked in to the hotel and entered my small room. Yellow rose petals had been sprinkled across the white bedspread. Yellow roses have many meanings. One is the promise of a new beginning. Another is: remember me.

My retreat to the mountains wasn't about letting go of Mark; I had done that gradually over many years. The retreat was about reflecting on my life with and without Mark. Yet I sensed something bigger was about to begin.

That night in the dining room, I had my first meal at the hotel. It was the most peaceful and delicious meal I had eaten in years.

When I fell asleep, I dreamt of walking on a stone path across a body of water. Water is a symbol of creation and life.

The next morning, I joined a hike organized by the hotel. I met the group by the van that would drive us to the start of the path. The hike leader turned to introduce herself; her name was Julia.

I felt an immediate connection to her because we shared a name. We chatted a bit, and I told her my husband had died two weeks ago. She announced to the group that she would drop them off and hike with me alone.

Julia was more than a hiking guide; she became a mentor. We walked for two hours together. She was widowed about seven years earlier. She listened to me tell my story and advised me in so many ways. She looked after me the rest of the week.

My two-week-old wound was fresh and raw. I needed to turn my attention to healing my wound. I needed to be gentle with myself and continue accessing my feelings.

I had multiple roles while caring for Mark. Now the focus was on me.

I was journeying back in time to move toward the future. There were continuous endings, large and small, all through Mark's illness and dying.

Now that he was gone, there would be continuous beginnings. It was time to renew my engagement in the world around me. My search became not who am I without Mark but who am I with others.

I would grow into my new self only by confronting all my grief. A new life would emerge, but what that life would be, I didn't know.

On Friday night, I read the Kaddish and said Mark's name aloud overlooking the mountains. At the end of reciting the Kaddish, I remembered that Mark had spent eighteen years in Raleigh. In Judaism, eighteen is a spiritual number, signifying life. He had a beautiful life in Raleigh.

When I first arrived, the mountaintop was wrapped in fog. I could barely see a few feet in front of me. Each day, it cleared a bit more, and the days became sunnier. By the last day, there wasn't a cloud in the sky.

On the last night, I had this dream:

Mark is sitting in his chair. I'm near him. We look out the large window and see hundreds of men, women, and children standing shoulder to shoulder. They are solemn-faced and holding candles.

They try entering our house. I push them back. Their supervisor hasn't arrived yet to oversee their actions. The supervisor arrives, though I can't see who it is; it's just known.

Everyone is inside the room sitting around Mark and me. They are writing on paper using wax that is dripping from their candles. I move around to observe. It's peaceful. I see a child without legs attached to a board; she's being cared for by an adult woman. I pick up the child and hand her to the woman. Everyone disappears. I sit down and write something with the candle wax for Mark. He watches from his chair.

PART

V

FALL 2014:
AFTER MARK'S DEATH

CHAPTER SIXTY-FOUR

Songs I Listened to After Mark Died

A SONG CAN BE so soothing; I want to rub it all over my body.

"Farewell My Angel" by Billy Joel

"Your Lone Journey" by Doc Watson

"For All I Know" by Donny Hathaway

"Blackbird" by the Beatles

"Glitter in the Sky" by Pink

"If It Be Your Will" by Leonard Cohen, sung by Antony

"Sit with Me," "Find Me," "Fire in the Rain" by Holly Near

"Tonight We'll Be Fine" by Leonard Cohen, sung by Teddy Thompson

"Come Away with Me" by Norah Jones

"Sunrise" covered by Eva Leach

"Feeling Good" by Nina Simone

"Rawhide" by various bluegrass musicians

DREAM: I'm sitting in a sling attached to a pulley. I can release a rope and glide down to the bottom floor or up to the ceiling. I can be inside or outside the home structure. I'm wearing a long silver satin robe that flows down into pools of water. The water absorbs into the satin robe I am wearing in slow motion. I'm now twelve feet above the ground. I begin to fold the long robe into puddles of water, asking: "Where are you, Mark?"

I spot a lilac-colored cocoon in a cloudlike clump with wormy things multiplying within it. Flower decorations line the banisters. It's day; it's night. I see people I know; I see people I don't know.

CHAPTER SIXTY-FIVE

The Mailbox Dream

MARK WAS TALKING TO me while leaning heavily against our mailbox in our front yard. I strained to hear his words. It was hard to hear because of some noise around me. He was wearing khaki shorts, a hat, and a black and white Hawaiian shirt. The shirt was tucked in.

He leaned against the mailbox the entire time.

The next morning, I walked into the kitchen and told David about my dream. He listened and continued eating breakfast. Not the most amazing dream.

Jeremy and Jenn arrived about fifteen minutes later to drop off Noah. As they walked in, Jeremy asked, "What happened to your mailbox?"

David, Jeremy, Jenn, and I ran outside. There was my mailbox lying in the dirt. It had fallen off the post. David and I looked at each other, stunned. Jeremy and Jenn were surprised, too, once I told them my dream!

Message from Mark: I'm communicating with you, Julia! You've got mail!

Love is the conduit! The signals are out there! Be open and aware and enjoy the love calls!

Shortly after this dream, I had my first visit with Maureen, a social worker at hospice. Her specialty is the grief process after a family member passes away.

I parked my car and walked to the grief counseling center. I noticed a modern-looking kinetic sculpture on the grass outside the building. It had the words "Cosmic Post" welded on it.

Maureen was waiting for me in the lobby. She extended her hand and smiled warmly. As I stepped into her office, I noticed there were dozens of butterflies artfully arranged on the walls, as if flying en masse to the heavens. We took our seats across from each other. There were also books on shelves, papers on the desk, stones with comforting words on them, and an assortment of artistic cards with images of healing.

"Where is Mark?" I asked. That is how we started my first session.

Toward the end of our session, I told her my dream about Mark leaning on our mailbox and finding it in the dirt the next morning. I asked Maureen about the sculpture outside. She said it was a type of mailbox where people can leave messages for loved ones who have passed on. There is a small container for letters, photos, or whatever someone wants to send. The smaller drawer below the container can be lit. The messages burn, and smoke is released into the air. My imagination is connected to my desires. Mark will hear from me via this magical mailbox. He had already revealed a message days earlier in my dream.

I was meeting the right people at right time to help me along my journey, like Julia at the hotel, and now Maureen.

Cosmic Post by Mike Roig, sculptor

CHAPTER SIXTY-SIX

No Longer

MARK IS NOW SPOKEN about in the past tense, even by his mother, Doe. How can that be? He was such a Here and Now personality when alive. He will forever be, as we move forward with our own lives, in the past tense. It's a little thing yet huge.

I received a text from a friend asking how the family was doing. I responded "fine," that I was heading to my grandson's first birthday party. Before I sent the text, I hesitated. Am I supposed to say "my" grandson now, or "our" grandson? I decided to say "my grandson." It made me feel sad.

I was no longer part of a "we." I was on my own. My focus was now finding the life that suits me. I was getting ready to put my house on the market. I needed a new view out my window.

The van, wheelchair, stair lift, and scooters had been sold or donated.

David listed the van on Craigslist. It was not a happy sale. We were contacted by a family whose nineteen-year-old son had been diagnosed with a neurological disease. The disease was progressing quickly, and they needed an accessible van.

The day we met to make the exchange, the father cried on my shoulder. Through his tears and disbelief, he told me his son was playing basketball less than a year earlier, and now isn't walking at all. David and I were silent as we drove off together.

DREAM: Mark is fully dressed lying on his back. He "comes to." His eyes remain closed, but he has a sweet smile on his face. I am given a special square box with openings on both ends. I place the box over his eyes. For a few treasured seconds I look into Mark's eyes, and he looks into mine.

DREAM: Doe, the kids, and I are at the cemetery. Mark's casket is visible. Someone asks him if he can take a "selfie."

i wait

silently
in bed
sinking
into myself
creating
an inner
stillness

the air
is unmoving,
my body
still
remembering
you

you
lying
still
still in your
grave

the bark outside
is ashen
the branches
are stark
the fallen
leaves
have
scattered

CHAPTER SIXTY-SEVEN

California

I WAS INVITED TO our friends Bill and Diane's son's wedding in San Francisco. I decided to make it a two-week trip and visit family and friends throughout California. David flew with me, stayed the weekend, and then flew back to Raleigh. He didn't want me to fly alone. We took a walk through Golden Gate Park and came upon a giant tree growing out of a huge rock. It was not rooted in its natural place, the earth. I identified with this strong tree and the solid rock. Mark was my earth, where I grew naturally. Now, alone, I would have to grow from someplace else and remain strong.

At the wedding, I danced with the single ladies group. We made our own little circle. A different circle for me.

"Are you dating yet?" a divorced woman asked.

Her question was unexpected but refreshing. I covered my face with my hands, stumbled out a few words.

"Not yet," I managed.

I was surprised by her question but was later told by a friend that single women ask this of other single women frequently. It's part of the new single life.

Mark and I met serendipitously at my cousin Laurie's wedding in LA in 1980. I was studying painting and printmaking at Boston University. At the last minute, I decided to fly out for the ceremony and celebration. Mark had been invited by the groom two days before the wedding, having met him only ten days earlier at a racquetball club.

Mark and I met while standing near the hors d'oeuvres. We chatted a few minutes, and Mark was instantly smitten. Me, not so much. I had a boyfriend back in Boston. But when he picked me up from the Boston airport less than a week later, we had a ridiculous argument in the car. By the time we got to my home thirty minutes later, I had ended our relationship.

Laurie called and said Mark would like to see me the next time I was in LA. My winter break was a few months away. I chose to spend it in LA. We had our first date at the West End Garden restaurant in West LA. It was magical. We ended up spending each day of my six-week break together until I had to return to school. We stayed in touch through phone calls and letters. Mark visited me in Boston in the spring. Immediately follow- ing my graduation, in June 1981, I moved to LA. A few months later, I moved in with him. On July 4, 1982, we were married.

After the friends' son's wedding, Naomi, who lives in San Francisco, and I drove down Highway 1 to LA. We made stops at places that had meaning for Mark and me. Sand Dollar Beach in Big Sur was one of our favorites.

When we got to LA, Naomi and I went our separate ways. I visited with one of Mark's aunts and several of his cousins, my cousins, his brother and sister-in-law, and friends. I stood in front of his childhood home and walked the mountains he enjoyed biking and hiking in as a child.

Mark was ever-present throughout the trip. From the most northern spot in San Francisco to the most southern in LA, I collected small rocks and shells to bring back to Raleigh and place on Mark's gravesite. Each rock in my hand became a solid reminder of Mark. I found rocks in muddy lakes, on hiking trails, at beaches and coastal lookouts, in parks and gardens, and at his childhood home.

There was nothing particular about the rocks I chose. The rocks were not always the rocks on the clear path in full view. I reached for ones under the water's surface or just out of reach. Once I found them, I held them for a moment, to feel their weight and know their importance. They were brown from the muddy lake, gray in the mountains, white by the sandy beach, reddish along the garden path. They would sit upon green grass above where Mark lies deep in the ground.

Pieces of California. Fragments of memories. Like seeds from our roots at the beginning of our life together. These chipped and broken segments from a much larger form found a way into my palm, then to Mark's gravesite.

One of the friends I visited in LA said we spend the first two-thirds of our life bringing relationships into our life, wrapping our arms around new loves and friendships. Our last third of life is spent saying our goodbyes.

I returned from my trip and went alone to the cemetery with my rocks. The sun was shining when I left my home in Raleigh. As I approached Chapel Hill, the fog was thick. I put on my headlights and drove up the winding highway. I parked and took the bag of rocks with me. I walked to Mark. I opened the bag and placed my offering in a small grouping near his temporary nameplate. In all, I had collected fourteen rocks. I hadn't counted them until that moment. It had been fourteen weeks since Mark died.

Together, Mark and I created a whole. Mark had been chipped apart and removed from my body. When I left these small rocks at his gravesite, it was like leaving a fragment of myself chipped away.

I looked at the trees surrounding the graves. I looked back at the grass covering his grave with the rocks in a pile. I had expected to feel a flood of emotion. I didn't feel anything. The cemetery is simply where Mark is located. I find my emotions well up in places other than the cemetery. My deepest feelings can be triggered at the sight of his hat, hearing bluegrass music, or passing a restaurant we enjoyed together. Not his grave.

I was back at the hospice grief center to meet with Maureen. As I neared the end of the hour-long visit, I asked if she would walk the labyrinth with me. There is one across the parking lot from her office, down a small hill. I hadn't walked one since Mark and I were at Mayo Clinic three years earlier, on the day we received Mark's diagnosis.

The labyrinth was half in sun, half in shadow. I let Maureen lead. I followed five to six steps behind her. Her purple crepe skirt fluttered in the wind.

We made our way through the circular labyrinth, our two shadows moving like a timepiece. The birds chirped in the trees, and women laughed on a nearby bench. Sheep grazed on a hill beside us.

We made our way to the center without talking. There was a heart arranged in brick in the center of the labyrinth. Maureen stooped down and placed a pinecone there. A few tears sprang to my eyes.

After returning home, I remained under my bedcovers the rest of the day reading, daydreaming about Mark, reliving my thoughts and feelings about the cemetery.

The next morning, I awoke and removed my engagement and wedding rings. There's a little indentation on my wedding finger where the rings pressed against my skin for more than thirty-two years. The rings were part of my hand like the nails above them or the wrist bone below.

CHAPTER SIXTY-EIGHT

Clare

SHORTLY AFTER I TOOK off my rings, I found my new home.

I felt confident and eager to look at new properties. I knew what I wanted in my next home and redefined what I was looking for after touring numerous listings.

I saw an advertisement in a local magazine about a brand-new subdivision being built a few miles from my home. The moment I saw the advertisement, I jumped in my car and drove there. I walked through all the spec homes and fell in love instantly with the model called "Clare."

I returned with two friends that day. Each day after, for the next eleven days, I brought family or friends to walk through the model. I wanted dozens of opinions and advice from as many people as possible. I didn't want to make a blunder.

Every time I visited the model, I got more excited. It was easy for me to imagine living there. The open floor plan was cheery and full of light. I got excited about being able to build a home for myself from scratch.

As I built a new foundation on the lot, it was a mirror to the foundation I was building inside myself. A new life, a new chapter.

I was aware that my decision to build came just four months after Mark had passed away. I was not following the usual wisdom that you shouldn't make any major decisions for at least a year following the death of a loved one. I hesitated briefly before I moved forward, asking myself if I needed to follow the path others had taken.

Perhaps if Mark had died suddenly, I would have followed the one-year guidance before moving or making any major changes to my life. However, he had lived ten years with a fatal illness. We said goodbye many times. We discussed everything before his passing. I knew he wanted me to move and start a new life once he was gone.

The clarity of Mark's words sharpened in my mind.

DREAM: I'm walking down a narrow street at night. The buildings and street are black. I turn and notice another street that is on a slight incline. Three people are staring at me. I feel like this street could lead me to Mark, but I can't walk up the hill.

I turn the other way and enter a train without walls. I exit in Mobile, Alabama, and double over crying hysterically. I can barely breathe, and my throat is clogged with tears.

Mark appears. He's making me laugh hysterically like he always did. It feels so good and is so much fun. He hugs me; it feels nice to be hugged. He turns his face, sits cross-legged, and floats away.

I had this dream the night I fell in love with the "Clare." During my next session with Maureen, I asked her about my dream. She answered that images of new and unfamiliar landscapes are common metaphors during grief. People are finding themselves in new terrain.

When I left Maureen's office, I spotted a small red heart pin on the ground. It made me smile. That same night while I was watching a movie with David, a character was wearing the same red heart on his lapel.

By the time I had found the house I wanted, I felt alert to my feelings, my independence, and relationships with my children and grandchildren. There were times I was doubling up on my role as a mother so I could do what Mark would do as a father. David was living with me and watching football one afternoon. I sat near him as he watched. Mark would have watched the game with him, and I didn't want David to watch alone.

CHAPTER SIXTY-NINE

Thanksgiving

From left to right, top row: David, James, Jeremy; bottom row: Emily, Max, me, Jenn, Noah, and Dœ, November 2014.

I WAS STILL LIVING in my old home, and the holidays were approaching. I decided to host Thanksgiving. Mark's words guided me: life continues, and stay close. My family and I felt in good spirits that afternoon. We decided to take a quick photo before we sat down for the meal. No one told anyone where to stand. Once the photo was printed, we all saw the blank space behind me. The space where Mark would have stood. The emptiness is loud. I can practically see the outline of his body.

Two days after Thanksgiving, Emily, Doe, and I drove to the cemetery together. The thirty-five-minute drive is the right amount of time to mentally prepare for the visit. As we got closer, our chatter quieted down, and we were all looking for the inconspicuous sign marking the cemetery by the side of the road. We made the left turn and drove as close as we could to Mark's burial spot. I parked the car, and we got out.

Emily stood on my left and Doe to my right. I noticed the grass was fuller and greener over Mark's grave. My fourteen rocks were still there, circling his temporary nameplate.

We were now arm in arm, our three distinct shadows against the sunlit grass, Emily's curls and Doe's signature beret in sharp silhouette. We laughed and cried and leaned into each other even tighter. Doe began to speak and was on a roll, gathering up and telling a mix of stories filled with sadness and humor. She unloaded every feeling. The words she was saying were strung together just right. I was in awe:

Mark was wonderful. He was full of love; he loved us all. He never had a down face. All we have now are memories and pictures. Mark made you feel good. He was a gem inside and out. Emily, you're the spitting image of him. He loved you, Julia, and me. Just read his book! It's all in there.

When you're out here, you know what's important. The small things don't matter. He knows we're here.

I certainly had a happy life. Neither Mark nor Richard got into horrible things or trouble. When things bothered them, it got straightened out and discussed with me. There was never any mishegas[17] or anguish. Everything went smoothly except once when Danny and I went to Hawaii. When we got home, we found out Mark had jumped from the roof into the pool . . . nothing much!

As adults they were busy with getting their acts together, jobs, and that kind of thing. Mark was working for Danny; Richard went into teaching. There was never any bickering. Whenever Mark and Richard got together, they had a great time.

Time waits for no one. Take a look at Noah. He pulls himself up, he'll be walking soon!

This is sad for me, to have my son die. This is sad for you, Julia, to lose your husband, and Emily, to lose your father, it's terribly sad.

I moved to Raleigh on Thanksgiving Day four years ago. Mark didn't tell me anything, maybe because I had been passing out quite a bit since Danny died. It must have been high anxiety. Anxiety can do strange things to you.

It's one of the hardest things you can face: losing your husband, your son, and your sister. I sit in my chair and cry every night thinking of Danny, Mark, and my sister Betty. Betty and I were so close; I spoke to her every day of my life. Sometimes several times a day. She always encouraged me, always had something to say to lift me up. She was more than a best friend. Betty was wonderful. She and Len [Betty's husband] adored Mark. Mark built the fence around their house. He helped them in so many ways. He used to ride his bike to my mother's apartment and ask what he could do to help her. He was something, something for the books!

Mark was so dear and thoughtful. I could talk to him; he always had an answer and always encouraged me. You can cry, I guess I'm letting my feelings out, what it is is unreal, it doesn't seem possible. How did it happen? Did it?

I look at his picture and think, Why? Why? Why?

---

17   *Mishegas* is a Yiddish term meaning "craziness."

He was the apple of our eye, I'll tell ya. He was the light in everyone's life. He had instant everything!

If Danny knew, he'd be torn up by this, beside himself.

As Mark faced his disease, he was brave, still smiling. Mark was suffering PLENTY. Then and there he was thinking of everyone else.

I didn't want to put any pressure on him. I didn't ask him questions. I remember seeing him with one cane, then two. Then he was in a wheelchair. There was nothing like that in our family, never any strange diseases. I thank God at least I lived here and got to spend time with him while he was ill. I'd sit near him. He always had a smile.

Those two babies gave him a lift. The kids were there every weekend. They were thinking of their father, not themselves. That was wonderful.

Julia, I remember when you first talked to me about this disease. You were very serious. We were at Topsail Beach a couple Thanksgivings ago. You explained everything to me. You sure have been strong through this. You were living with this, facing this each day. Everybody, including your kids and Richard, feels bad. No one feels like you feel. We feel the worst, you and me. You go about your day, your life, your this and your that. But it never leaves you. Nobody wants to lose their husband or their son. Nobody wants to accept death. It's there, but why think about it?

When it's there you think about it, and when they're gone you really think about it!

You meet different people and they're nice . . . but you don't dwell on them. You just ask, "When did you say you were leaving?"

How do you go forward? It's not easy. I'm here.

I can't do anything.

I can't call him and say, "Come over for a tuna sandwich." And that makes me feel awful. It's so final. That's why so many things are insignificant. They don't mean a thing.

My mother-in-law Esther would say, "Children are lent to you."

There isn't a day that goes by I don't think about Mark. My thoughts never go away from Mark. They're all good thoughts, and there's no anguish because everything was always good.

I worked as a secretary for him for about a year. I enjoyed that.

But you have to control yourself and talk to yourself and tell yourself there's nothing you can do about it. Wishing, wishing, wishing I could hear his voice. Thanksgiving dinner was delicious and beautiful, but there was a missing piece, Mark. As soon as I got there, I was thinking of him and wanting to hold his hand.

WINTER MONTHS:
LETTING GO

CHAPTER SEVENTY

December

AFTER CONSULTING WITH FAMILY and friends about selling my house and moving to a new home, I decided to purchase the lot in the new subdivision. It would be the first time I would sell and buy a house on my own. The final appointment with the realtor to buy my new home was scheduled for two o'clock on a Tuesday in December 2014.

I had been visiting with friends from my old art studio downtown, and I drove north along Glenwood Avenue to get to the meeting. I knew I'd be passing Mark's old office. I saw it on my left and quickly turned into the parking lot. I found a spot by the woods, the same wooded view Mark had from his office.

I sat in my car looking at the trees. I placed my hands on each side of my face and curled them into fists. I began pulling Mark into my mind, reaching for his presence. I wanted him to know what I was about to do. I was wondering if he'd agree with my decision. I pulled him, his being into my being. Giant tears poured down my face. I continued searching the woods and talking aloud to Mark through my tears, explaining my plans, trying hard to hear his answers.

I turned to view the parking lot. I remembered walking with Mark through the lot toward his office dozens of times when he was well and working. I pictured Mark sitting in his office, these woods behind him through the large pane of glass.

Twenty minutes passed before I turned the car on and continued my drive north. When I got to the site of my new home, I pulled into the parking lot outside the sales office. My agent, Carole, met me there. Three hours later, the offer was set.

This is what Mark had told me to do before he died. I disagreed with him at the time, yet now I knew he was right. I had turned a corner. The construction started right away. I was given a July move-in date.

Later in December, hospice held a service called "A Night of Remembrance, Lights of Love." Memorial placards printed with personal messages were placed at the base of dozens of luminarias outside along the walkways.

The words I selected for Mark's placard read, "We miss you every day. We love you every day." The glow of luminarias in the dark and rainy night was beautiful.

Inside the warm auditorium, a service was held for families who had lost a loved one. I sat with Doe, Jeremy, and Emily on the aisle a couple rows from a makeshift altar. There were sprigs of rosemary, symbolizing remembrance, in a basket, along with bells and candles on the table in front. As we waited for the service to begin, music was playing, and a nature slide show appeared on two large screens in front of us.

The service included singing, readings, and sharing of names. A micro-phone was passed up and down the rows. Each person in the auditorium said the name of the person they were remembering. As the microphone was handed to our group, Emily and Jeremy each stated, "My dad," Doe said, "My son," and I ended with, "My husband."

In front of Mark's luminaria, December 2014.

My neighbor was hosting their yearly holiday party. Mark and I had skipped the last few because of his illness. This year, as part of my new philosophy of saying yes to every invitation, I decided to attend. Life is a continuous improvisation; there is no script. The first rule of improv acting is to always respond by saying, "Yes, and . . ." I was learning life only happens after saying yes. In many ways, yes was the way Mark had always lived.

I wore a sparkly gold sweater and earrings, grabbed a small clutch, and headed over to the party on foot. It was a cold night. I saw familiar faces as I entered my neighbor's kitchen. I had begun chatting with someone I knew when another neighbor came over and stood close to me.

After a fast minute of small talk, she blurted out that if she were to die and her husband was left alone, she'd want him to remarry. She repeated this sentence with an oversized smile and nervous chuckles.

"Will you remarry?" She continued her spastic chuckling.

I became lightheaded, choked a bit on a cashew, and sat down on the nearest barstool.

"Mark and I talked about me dating; he wanted me to," I answered weakly. "I'll be right back."

I walked over to where the drinks were, picked up a mug of brandy-laced eggnog, and downed a couple Jell-O shots. I returned to the barstool and resumed talking to my neighbor. I wanted to hear what she had to say. She continued speaking, unfiltered. She spoke about her mother's passing right before their eldest child was born, and her father before her next child was born. "We told stories about them, but they don't know their grandparents. Your grandchildren won't know Mark," she said, looking me in the eye. "They just won't! All the stories won't matter." She jabbed my arm to punctuate her words.

I got up and got another brandy-laced eggnog.

A widow is a walking Rorschach test. People project their fears and insecurities on you. I was learning I had to be prepared. I needed to protect myself. I made my way through the crowd, getting sympathetic looks, a thumbs-up, a heavy arm on my shoulder. It's all good, I suppose. People trying their best.

After Mark died, I held our last annual Hanukkah party in our home. We lit dozens of menorahs across our dining room table as Jeremy welcomed everyone. We ate beef brisket and potato latkes. The children took turns being the emcee during the talent show. Everyone went all out with their singing, dancing, magic tricks, stories, and jokes.

I lit a memorial candle and placed it on the mantel by a photo of Mark. It was a photo we had taken of him during an earlier talent show, when he was well. He's standing up playing his banjo.

Mark at the Hanukkah party.

In the middle of all the holiday celebrations, I also needed to find a seller's agent. It was a painstaking decision. Selecting the right agent weighed heavily on my shoulders. I interviewed five agents, all by myself.

Looking back, I should have had someone with me. You need another set of eyes and ears. I walked blindly into an important decision and didn't even know it.

I began sorting through the stuff in my home. What an ordeal! I tossed out, gave away, dropped off at Goodwill, and sold on Craigslist all the accumulated furniture, books, knickknacks, clutter, and clothing that filled our home. I was packing up an entire life!

Everything came off my walls. I didn't stop. At times I was a machine. It was easy to toss out the excess, the fat of my belongings. At other times, the purging and throwing away felt like a betrayal. The things I was getting rid of had belonged to Mark. We had built every aspect of our life and our home together. And, just like Mark, certain mementos felt larger than life. I sifted through memories. What should I do with his glasses, the Swiss army knife from his childhood? The three-by-five-inch booklets of the Declaration of Independence and the Constitution he kept in his bedside table during our entire marriage? Artifacts from an illness: the blood pressure cuffs and notebook with his daily account of his blood pressure, written in his handwriting? The expired medications and bags of swabs?

I felt torn apart by having to separate from these items. On one day, the anxiety and tension got a hold of me, and I took half a Tranxene and lay down a few hours. Even after the medication and the rest, I still couldn't return to the task.

After stopping for a few days, I found it easier to let go of Mark's things. He had an extensive collection of Civil War history books. I held each one in my hands, turned it over, and flipped through the pages briefly. I wasn't going to read them. I laid each one in a box and sealed it up with tape. All his books on healing, patient advocacy, neurology, preventive medicine, all went away. Like a curator, I sorted through the items, weighing their meaning. If a positive feeling or memory was sparked, it stayed.

As I continued packing, I found a small six-by-nine-inch music box for jewelry. Mark had bought it for me years ago. The cover is a reproduction of a piece of Tiffany stained glass. It has purple wisteria and yellow leaves. I hadn't seen this music box in years.

I opened it and found a dozen or so unmatched earrings. They were pretty. I remembered as I studied each one that I didn't have the heart to toss them just because their other half had been lost. Perhaps I'd find some use, turn them into a necklace, a brooch, or add a unique flair to a picture frame. I saw each earring sparkle and shine in the velvet-lined box, missing its perfectly matched other.

I also laid out his clothing for Jeremy, Emily, David, and James to go through. The unused clothes hanging in his closet made me sad. It was time to let them go. The four of them entered our bedroom at different times during an afternoon and came out with a small pile of Mark's belongings. It felt good to see the assorted hats, ties, and scarves in their hands. David ended up with the tie Mark had worn when we first met. I never wore Mark's wedding band on a chain around my neck. I offered it to David as a ring he may like to wear when he marries. He tried it on his ring finger. It fit perfectly.

I chose to keep Mark's brown suede jacket, a pair of winter gloves, and a cream-colored hat. I kept all the photos but planned on just putting out a few in my new house. I wasn't interested in creating a shrine.

I was ready to streamline and head in a new direction. Getting rid of my beloved dining room set and other furnishings was easier than anticipated. The biggest loss was Mark. Everything else was just things.

DREAM: I catch an insect in a jar. I bring the jar into my room and release it. I understand in my dream someone is going to enter my room and become impregnated by the insect. A crowd arrives to watch. I let the crowd in and hug them, yet I am careful when I open the door to not let the insect escape.

CHAPTER SEVENTY-ONE

December 31, 2014

I RECEIVED SEVERAL INVITATIONS for New Year's Eve. I chose to stay home alone. I drank lemon ginger tea, let chocolates melt in my mouth, and packed boxes. I watched two movies back-to-back. Both were about widows. They were cathartic to watch. One was called *The Face of Love*, the other *Elsa and Frank*. The most touching scene from *The Face of Love* was when the character Annette Benning played believed she had seen her dead husband, and she returns to the same spot day after day, in the hope of catching another glimpse.

I'd wait hours or days on a bench, too, if I knew I'd see Mark appear.

At midnight, alone, I said goodbye to 2014. I left Mark there. He wouldn't join me in 2015.

Moonlight

Awakened by moonlight
through my window
I step out of bed and open the shutters
The sky is black, the full moon luminous
A high beam, glaring, blaring white
I stare at the moon and think of Mark
The moon begins to grow
like a dream amid dancing stars
Its whiteness cold against the dark sky
I watch the moon sink into tall trees
Soon, it's gone
Erased by early sunlight
The sun is warm and demanding
Erasing my reverie

CHAPTER SEVENTY-TWO

Discovery

DAVID HELPED PHOTOGRAPH AND place all the furniture I wanted to sell on Craigslist. I was debating whether to keep Mark's recliner chair. It's comfy and soft yet clunky and unattractive. Mark had asked me to sell it; he thought it would remind me of his illness and sad times.

I was sitting on the recliner trying to decide what to do. I reached down into a side pocket. I pulled out the hospice booklets and sheets of paper from the speech therapist. She had typed up phrases for him, ones he came up with, to point to as a way of communicating after losing his ability to speak.

As I read the list, I felt visited by Mark. I heard his voice. It read like a poem:

Mark Freifeld: 10 commonly used phrases and sentences:
1. I love you.
2. This disease is a pain in the ass.
3. That's an issue.
4. That's a classic.

5.   I hate when that happens.
6.   I could really go for a hickory burger.[18]
7.   She's simply adorable.
8.   Don't take no for an answer.
9.   Where do you want to eat?
10.   I love the people in my life.

I decided to keep his chair and not sell it on Craigslist.

---

18   A burger from one of Mark's favorite restaurants in LA called the Apple Pan.

CHAPTER SEVENTY-THREE

Unsteady

WITHOUT MARK, THERE WAS no buffer between me and the world. I was bumping up and ramming into areas of life I didn't understand. It was a whirlwind of meetings with real estate agents, stagers, painters, home inspectors, and handymen, as well as packing, selling, moving, and storing all the stuff. Mark had always protected me from those hard edges. He was a salve, soothing all my wounded feelings. Life felt coarser without him.

One night, I burst into uncontrollable laughter in front of David. All the papers from my shredder spilled all over the room while I hastily tried to empty it into a big trash bag. It was a mess. I didn't understand my reaction. I felt unhinged; the laughter was too wild.

I called my cousin Clarey, and she said uncontrolled laughter is a relief valve. Considering all the time I was spending worrying, trying to control everything happening around me while I conducted a major life makeover, I should laugh with abandon. She told me I wouldn't fall apart if I let the wild laughter out. She added: enjoy the process, do what feels good, you are in charge, and the best part, there is no wrong answer!

The next day I pretended I was at a spa. I went to my gym and exercised. I rested on my couch and barely moved from it. Psychologically, I had to shift into neutral. Unwind, reset, no pressure; coast through the day. I began preparing a slow-cooking beef stew. I thought about making an appointment to see my grief counselor, Maureen. Richard, Mark's brother, was arriving in town in a few days, and I didn't need to be falling apart.

The day after I did my slowdown, a doozy of an anxiety attack kicked in while I was driving to meet a friend. We were going to see the METLive opera *The Merry Widow*. Perhaps, I joked, I'd pick up a few tips from watching the opera. By the time I pulled into the parking lot, the anxiety attack was full blown. I downed a full Tranxene tablet and reclined my driver's seat. I told my friend to go in and get seats for us.

I rested for fifteen minutes or so, then went into the theater and found my friend. I fell asleep during the opera because of the drug. I opened my eyes briefly and read the subtitles. I thought it said the singer was getting nervous about paying all the bills. I thought, I can relate! I fell back to sleep.

I was beginning to experience and understand the difference between anxiety and depression. With anxiety, you can move forward. Depression keeps you stuck and unmoving.

I was struggling, but I was moving forward.

Nameplate

RICHARD ARRIVED A COUPLE days later. We were having a dedication ceremony for Mark at the temple where we were installing a nameplate on a wall in the sanctuary. It was one week shy of the six-month anniversary of Mark's passing.

The nameplate has his name in English and Hebrew, and birth and death dates. It was made of brass with the letters and numbers raised. Next to his name is a light bulb in the shape of a flame. It glows orange when on. It will be lit each year on the anniversary of his passing.

The assistant rabbi led the short service. He spoke with humor and love about Mark. He recited prayers and led us in a couple of songs. It was intimate and tender. Tears flowed down my cheeks.

While I held Noah in one arm, I reached with my free hand to touch the bulb and turn it on. Mark's name glowed in the warm light.

DREAM: It is the six-month anniversary of Mark's passing. The rabbi is going to lead us in a ritual. I arrive early without wearing shoes. There are many rooms, large and small. I enter one of the rooms. The rabbi says, "We are going to dance to mark the moment." I dance with a person then wander into another room. I notice my shoes are missing again. This happens three times in the dream.

Mark appears, ghostlike. He does not touch the ground and moves in the breeze like a Chinese paper lantern.

He looks at me, and I begin sobbing. I stretch out my arms to reach him and touch him. Richard is behind me. He places his arms around my waist to hold me back. Mark's image moves behind me. I look in front of me, yet see him behind me, as if I am looking in a rearview mirror.

CHAPTER SEVENTY-FIVE

Natural Feelings

And the day came when the risk to remain in the bud was more painful
than the risk it took to bloom.
—ANAIS NIN

WHILE MY NEW HOUSE was being constructed, I began having doubts
about selling my home. The home was rich with memories of life and
death. My new house was a blank slate filled with my future.

I cried every day for several weeks after signing the contract to build
my new home and sell our old one. The commotion of repair jobs on my
old house continued. I was writing checks and getting estimates. Fear and
doubt bubbled up daily. I was fretful and began experiencing shortness of
breath. My throat felt tight, and I was often hyperventilating while driving.

What will happen to all my memories of raising our children together
with Mark? Would they go away in the same way all the things I had
thrown away had disappeared?

The house and Mark merged into one. I began to believe that if I left
my home, I'd be leaving Mark. I had known I'd be busy getting the house
prepared for sale, and it would be complicated, but I didn't expect the
emotional outpouring. When my emotions poured out, it was like a storm,
and I was pounded with rain and thunder.

Everything in my life was shifting: people, places, and things. I was living a life where I was experiencing a continuous feeling of letting go, letting go, letting go, all the while heading into the unknown.

Mark and I sold three homes together; he made it a bundle of laughs each time. He buffered any worries I may have had. I didn't feel the weight of responsibilities with those home sales that I felt now. The jokes weren't happening like they would have if Mark had been there with me.

I felt alone and anxiety-ridden. The seller's agent was a disappointment. He would take days to reply to my questions. He was completely unavailable. One afternoon, I began talking stream-of-consciousness-style to a handyman I had met two days earlier about the cost of replacement windows and missing my husband.

"He died last July. What would he want me to do? My realtor is my realtor, not a therapist. I understood that. But he should know to reply to my texts because I'm anxious. I'm trying to keep it a business relationship, but selling my home is tied up with so many emotions. My house will be listed in three days. Is it the right price?" I rambled on, jumping from topic to topic.

I burst into tears and looked nervously around the room. He opened his arms wide, and I fell into them. He held me and I sobbed. I let it all go.

After I calmed down, he released me from his arms. I felt better.

He asked how my husband died. I briefly described MSA. He cringed. It is cringeworthy.

That night I sent an email to Maureen, the subject line simply: SOS. I met with her a few days later.

In the midst of turmoil and mourning, yearning and missing Mark, I wondered what kind of changes were sweeping in. What will I embrace? How do I adapt? If I take steps forward, does that further remove me from Mark?

"If you could tell something to the earlier Julia, the Julia that cared for Mark three to five years ago, what would you tell her?" Maureen asked.

"Trust all your instincts. You know yourself. Be kind to yourself and continue feeling joy." I answered without hesitation.

I decided to plunge into this growth process. The questions and uncertainties were inescapable. Staying stuck seemed pointless. I had to evolve. Life had a hand on my back pushing me ahead. I knew periods of anxiousness would come and go. The goal was to find joy each day with my children, grandchildren, and friends.

I knew my house would eventually sell and I'd be living in my new home. I needed another ritual to mark the transition of leaving one home and moving to another. So I walked through each room of our home. I had lived there nineteen years. Our children were twelve, ten, and five when we moved in.

If our home had a voice, it would say, "I held your family here. I had openings and exits, windows to gaze out of. There were places to play, sing, dance, watch movies, eat, and talk. You played in the snow in the front yard. You grilled and gathered on the back deck. There were rooms here for being alone and crying. I surrounded all of you and protected you. I stood here and was painted colors, wallpapered, hammered into, tiled, carpeted, and walked on."

The house needs to know I didn't love it at first. It took a while for me to feel at home. Eventually, I put my stamp on it, filling it with my paintings, photos, and furnishings. The most crucial thing that happened was that our family grew there and created life there. I came to love it.

After one visit with our rabbi, she and I were standing by our front door. She paused, looked slowly around the entryway, and said a prayer in Hebrew. She explained the prayer's translation: "God is in this place."

Our home had good times and good vibes. It also contained our family's largest tragedy. Throughout all the moments, our home felt loving, peaceful, and welcoming. Something special, like God or love, filled our home.

CHAPTER SEVENTY-SIX

Autopsy

IN MARCH 2015, EIGHT months after Mark died, I received the copy of his final pathology report. The first line read "Final Diagnosis: Multiple System Atrophy." The report was two pages of detailed medical information describing all the ways Mark's brain had atrophied.

One line stood out. The functions relating to emotions, cognition, memories, perceptions, and decision-making were all "relatively preserved." I wasn't surprised. He used to say, "I feel smarter than ever!" He and I had communicated nonverbally for months before he died. I could interpret the subtle movement of a finger, a raised eyebrow, an assortment of smiles and nonsmiles. I read his eyes perfectly; each delicate facial expression conveyed full paragraphs of ideas and feelings.

I had wanted to know what the hell he went through, and now I did. It felt like another message from Mark.

When Mark became ill, he wore earbuds all the time, whether they were plugged into a device or not. He often fell asleep with them in his ears. I never questioned his wearing them. I imagined he was listening to something beyond what we could hear. Now, I had to listen to beyond what was in front of me. I needed to tune in to Mark's signals and continue what we practiced, nonverbal communication.

"Embrace the mystery" was my latest mantra.

CHAPTER SEVENTY-SEVEN

Moments

I WENT TO PURCHASE a printer by myself. I selected one after asking a young salesman several questions. I felt good about my purchase. While standing by the cash register, the young salesman asked for my phone number. He asked if I was related to Mark Freifeld. He turned his computer so I could see what he could see. I saw Mark's name in all capital letters, along with his email and our home address. Tears filled my eyes.

I attempted to answer. "Well, yes, I mean that is my husband's name. He passed away last July." I stopped talking. I couldn't speak. As I reached for a Kleenex in my purse, I asked him to remove Mark's name and email. He told me he could remove the email but not the name. I drove home and got under the covers. I listened to music, read, and napped.

After getting up, I got myself ready to head to an International Folk Dance Club at a nearby park. There were fluorescent lights on the ceiling and quick-paced Bulgarian music playing over the speakers. I stepped in alone, wearing black from head to toe. The women there were wearing wildly colored skirts and tops with bright sashes tied around their waists.

The men wore slacks, brightly colored shirts, and two belts around their waists. Many of the dancers wore embroidered pointy-toed moccasins. As the dancers spiraled across the room, one of the men grabbed my hand and led me through my first dance. It was awkward, but I was starting to learn my new dance steps.

SPRING 2015:
LEARNING TO COPE

CHAPTER SEVENTY-EIGHT

Support Groups

I MET WITH TWO groups in four days. The first group I attended was for single women over fifty-five. The other was a support group for widows. My mantra was to say yes to every invitation, so I went.

SINGLES MEETUP

I instantly felt out of place with the women involved in the Meetup group.

What am I doing here? I thought.

As soon as I sat down, a woman asked for my cell number. I said no. It was awkward for a second as she raised her eyebrows and quickly looked away from me. I felt it was too fast to ask for my cell, and I had gotten better with boundaries.

I kept my distance throughout the night. I listened to their conversations, observed their lives. They were all divorced. I warmed up to them by the end of the evening, but it wasn't my group.

BEREAVEMENT SUPPORT GROUP

Through hospice, I signed up for a widows support group that met once a week for eight weeks. I walked in feeling open, vulnerable, and right at home.

Including me, there were eight women sitting around a square table. There were folded name cards in front of each person. We communicated with soft smiles and quick glances at each other. "You'll understand me," was the unspoken message.

We waited silently for the facilitator to arrive.

It was a relief when she joined us at the table. She opened with a bit of business: forms for us to sign and a description of how the meetings would proceed. There were two rules to follow: no touching (patting someone can be a feeling-stopper) and no giving advice.

The only other support group I'd been in was the Well Spouse Association. It was unstructured. There were no formal rules or format to follow. People in that group were in the throes of caregiving, their stress palpable. And the discussion was whatever was on our minds that day.

The air in this group felt different. The day-to-day caregiving was over. The doctor appointments, treatments, procedures, far-flung hopes for recovery were over. The goodbyes and dying were behind us. That huge, complicated, consuming, frustrating tsunami of illness that crashed into our lives, drenching us and almost drowning us, was over.

Our lives were the quiet after the storm. We grappled not with death but with the long and lonely days we were now living and could imagine as our only future. We felt the slowness and stillness of time. Our futures were blank. There was emptiness surrounding us where once there had been a warm hand to hold, warm eyes to gaze into, and a warm voice to tell us we were loved.

I felt comfortable with these women. I identified with their loss and appreciated their struggle and courage to join the group. We were strangers.

Over the next eight weeks, we would know each other's grief, and intimately know each husband's life and death.

By being there, I got to honor Mark each week. I could remember, mourn, and praise him, express whatever I wanted with a lovely guide and fellow travelers.

Every meeting started with the facilitator, Terri, asking us to close our eyes and take a few moments and a few breaths. She'd hit a small gong and ask us to open our eyes. Next, one by one, around the table, we'd say our husband's name aloud. A single candle of two people embracing was lit in their memory. Then we'd go around the table again, describing in a few sentences how our previous week had been.

The first time I said Mark's name aloud to the group, it felt like a knife pierced my heart. I noticed the raw emotions and vulnerability in the other women, too, after mentioning their husbands' names. The simple structure of the opening of the meeting was enchanting. It created a mood for relaxation and revelation.

By the end of the first meeting, my imagination took flight. I pictured each husband appearing behind or seated next to his wife, each husband totally focused on her. These husbands would glance slightly at the group but were primarily looking at their wives. They were healthy men. Some were young, others older. They were at peace with themselves and out of pain. They were there for their wives. I felt Mark next to me. I was tempted to reach for his hand.

Each week, Terri led us in an activity. It was always something powerful to trigger our emotions and memories. During the second meeting, there were dozens of small objects on a table. We had a few seconds to grab something off the table. Don't think too hard, Terri told us; just notice an object that reminded us of our husband and pick it up. A few minutes later we took turns holding up the object and sharing our story. I selected a small red, fuzzy, sparkly ball.

"This looks like a little firework. We were married on the Fourth of July, and we had beautiful sparks throughout our marriage, all the way until the end," I said.

By the third week, we felt like we knew each other. Terri placed our small objects in a heart-shaped dish and centered it on the table near the candle. There was a tiny soccer ball, a rabbit's foot, a star, a small penguin, and other items. I spotted my little red sparkly ball. These visual reminders placed our husbands in the room with us.

She asked us what was unique in our lives after losing a spouse. The answers came easily from around the table:

- I'm redefining my role and identity.

- Half of me is missing.

- My personal cheerleader is gone.

- The person who knew me best is gone.

- The person I had future plans with is gone.

- The person who made me laugh the most is gone.

We ended each meeting with one or two words to describe how we felt. I noticed the language was shifting to include words of strength: determined, reaching out, grateful, supported, finding humor, seeing spring and sunnier days.

At the end of our meetings, Terri would hand out small pieces of paper with a poem or inspiring words, like this:

"Growing means we move from what we have been to what we are now and, hopefully, on into the future to what we will or can be. We are not just 'human beings' but 'human *becomings.*'"

I learned you can't rush a butterfly from inside the cocoon. The butterfly will emerge when it's ready. Our singular, independent, and, we hope, beautiful life will unfold. There is life after death. The women were having a deep effect on me. One morning, I awoke at 3:00 a.m. and suddenly had to draw their faces from memory.

The mood of the group swayed and shifted over time. There was more warmth and casual conversation between us while waiting for the fourth meeting to begin.

Each week, two women were given twenty minutes to discuss their husband in any way they'd like. The women brought in photos, awards, family crests, articles of clothing, and jewelry, letters, or a hobby-related item. When the women spoke, it felt holy. There was nothing casual, offhanded, sarcastic, or uncomfortable about it.

We were immediately drawn into each other's stories. As an item was taken out of a bag and placed on the table, there was usually a slight pause, a sigh as soft as a whisper. Here is my husband, and I'm going to share him with you. As the object circled the room, it was handled with the utmost care. As one of the women's favorite photos was released from her hand, her eyes followed as it was passed from person to person.

"This picture is us, the essence of our relationship," she said.

They were treasures, pieces of a full life being lovingly remembered. One woman brought in a cardboard pencil holder her husband had made with a dozen pencils he had sharpened. She hadn't touched it since he died. It was passed around the table as if it were a chalice used for sacramental wine.

My turn came during the fourth meeting. I had twenty minutes to distill the essence of Mark. I rehearsed at home with a timer. I brought in two items. The first was a bright orange T-shirt that Jeremy and Jenn made for Mark when they announced they were expecting. It lists, on the front and back, their favorite sixteen pieces of his advice. When they created the shirt, it was difficult for them to narrow down the advice he had given them. They would have needed several T-shirts to include ALL his advice! The T-shirt was fun and got a lot of laughs.

In addition, I brought the memoir Mark wrote. I lovingly read a few sections. I felt proud and happy that he had completed his book and I could share it. When I finished speaking uninterrupted, I felt both contentment and a sense of bittersweetness. I wanted to tell everyone sitting around the table: you've now heard about my best friend, my most beloved, the best part of my life.

The activity during the fifth meeting was wonderful. There were art postcards sprawled across the table. The paintings were emotionally evocative. They were painted with intense colors and dreamlike images of landscapes, faces, and figures. Again, Terri asked us to make a quick decision selecting one or two cards. Don't overthink the process, she said.

I snapped up two and sat back down. We took turns around the table describing what we saw in the paintings. I held up the first card. It was a portrait of a woman with her eyes closed and a desertlike landscape behind her. I projected myself onto it. I can close my eyes and be in my head a lot. I'm daydreaming, fantasizing, wishing, or simply moving away from reality. These feelings swirl and whirl inside my head. The thoughts feel so huge they seem to roam across the earth.

I held up and described the second card. There were two figures separated by a yellow streak. It reminded me of Mark and me. We are separated by death, yet he can still feel close by. The female face in the picture is in swirling cool water with her eyes open. That is me. I'm alive and identify with water. It is a life force.

The male face is in the earth, painted in earth tones: yellow, orange, and brown. Mark is in the earth now. He was always of the earth, strong and grounded. His eyes are closed, and his face is abstracted, transformed by death.

At the sixth meeting, there was a discussion on emptiness: empty space around us, empty hours and days. That hit a nerve. We have all dealt with loneliness and emptiness. One woman acknowledged that after being shut in during a three-day snowstorm, "I've always enjoyed my company, but there is such a thing as too much of a good thing."

Terri gave us a handout called "Six Types of Loneliness":

1. Interpersonal loneliness: the result of losing a significant, or intimate, relationship.

2. Social loneliness: where a person is on the fringes of a group, excluded from a group, or is actively rejected.

3. Cultural loneliness: a person belongs to a different culture and feels that they don't fit or belong in the new culture.

4. Intellectual loneliness: a person feels intellectually or educationally out of sync with their peers, their family, or social group.

5. Psychological loneliness: a person has experienced a trauma that separates them from others around them; it is something other people can't fully understand.

6. Existential or cosmic loneliness: an isolation experienced by a person who is facing death.

I was learning the vocabulary of grief. It's important to name something to understand it, see it, and feel it. Another tip from the evening: grief is a loving and sacred journey.

I left each meeting a different person than when I walked in. I was awakening to my new self. I began to understand that if I addressed the grief, it could be abated and not crush me. I let the experience happen and touch me deep inside. As a group, I felt we were mirroring each other's grief, and this allowed us to feel less alone. There was someone else sharing our pain, anger, worry, and sadness. We all agreed the grief process was one step forward, two steps back.

The other activity during the sixth meeting was stringing beads. All types of beads were laid out on the table. Some were made of crystal, others of stone, glass, silver, pearls, and wood. We worked silently while soothing music played in the background and heard the chime of beads as they were handled and removed from the plastic containers.

The repetitive motion of stringing beads calmed my nerves. Stringing beads led to stringing memories. I made two strands: one represented Mark, one represented me. I tied the ends of each one and strung a large purple teardrop-shaped bead and one turquoise bead down each of the cords. That was our matching base. I added beads with letters spelling out our names. My strand included pink and clear crystals, a red glass bead, and three emerald green beads. Mark's strand included a flat, round black bead, a solid white one, a silver one, and a speckled brick-colored one. I added a red glass one and three emerald ones on his like the ones on mine.

We matched and didn't match. The three emeralds represented our children; the two small turquoise ones represented our grandsons Noah and Max. Mark's was made of earthy colors and solid forms; my strand was made of crystals clear like the air, light, and water. I joined the two strands with a chain and turned it into a double-strand necklace.

By the seventh week, I felt like I knew everyone's husband intimately. I knew how they met their wives; I knew their hobbies, occupations, favorite foods, travels, friends, schooling, children, strengths. and weaknesses. I knew all about their illnesses and deaths.

The activity for the seventh week was walking the labyrinth as a group. Terri explained there is a difference between a maze and labyrinth. While walking through a maze, you have to make choices to find the right path. You can't get lost along a labyrinth. It's not a puzzle or difficult to navigate. Walking along a labyrinth can quiet the mind. The delicate turns and spirals bring you to the center and then back to the beginning.

This was the second time I had walked the labyrinth within a few months. I was surrounded by the other women yet felt alone as I entered. I pictured Mark on the nearby bench watching me, smiling, his sweet eyes looking at me. As I walked near the bench on one of the turns, I kept my eyes on it and felt him there. A few minutes later, I felt Mark was gone. Gone from my life. I felt totally alone. Each turn had new meaning. I was careful making those turns; I slowed down and watched my steps. When I arrived at the center, I saw the intermingled hearts created from brick and felt a sharp stab inside of me. I got lost and walked in circles for a moment. I couldn't figure out where the exit was. I crossed a few lines and eventually made my way out.

I looked over at the green hill beside the labyrinth. There was a metal structure that reminded me of a grave. I thought of Mark in his grave. I thought about his brain not being with his body. I was overwhelmed with sadness. The slow walk back to the room gave me time to detach from those feelings and switch gears. I have heard a healthy life includes forgetting. Withdrawing from the pain is a survival skill and a miracle. A hard miracle.

When we returned to the room, we made vision board collages from images and words torn out of magazines. What were our goals? What did we hope for our future? It was a breezy activity. I glued pictures of families having fun together, sunrises, hearts, and birds flying in the sky. I chose uplifting words and phrases: "jumpstart," "a new era," "taking wing," "cultivate your spirit," and "love."

Terri asked us what we did to release our frustrations, anger, or sadness. There were many expected answers: yoga, walking, knitting, and talking with a friend. An older, overall-wearing Southern farm gal surprised everyone when she said she had begun shooting aluminum cans with a gun. With a big smile, she said it was the best release of her emotions. She had never shot a gun in her life. The gun had belonged to her husband. He would pile up cans or bottles on a ledge and use them as targets.

I had never touched a gun in my life. The woman's description intrigued me. I was willing to try anything to unload my own pent-up emotions. I knew James's dad, John, had a gun, and after that meeting I asked him to show me how to shoot it. He agreed.

We met at the shooting range. John was patient as he explained what we were going to do, from putting on the ear and eye protective wear to holding the gun and loading the bullets.

I watched John shoot first. He showed me how to stand, aim, and pull the trigger. Then he loaded three bullets. I was given the gun a second time. I stood with my feet apart, my arms straight ahead holding the gun. I aimed for the bullseye. I pulled the trigger. At that instant, both of my eyes closed, and I felt an intense jolt through my body. As the bullet released, I opened my eyes. I had hit the bullseye. Wow! I had purchased a whole box of bullets, but after firing the three and hitting the center of the target, I said to John, "I'm done."

For our final meeting, we were asked to bring in our husband's favorite food. I was excited about this. Mark had many favorite foods: hamburgers, strawberry shortcake, and Caesar salad, to name a few. I decided on beef brisket and kasha. He loved my brisket so much he once wrote a humorous song about it!

The night of the meeting, I wore a shirt with sparkly hearts because food was love in our family. I hadn't made brisket in a long time, and I became emotional making it during the day. Not having meals together was a big loss for me when Mark was too ill to eat. Living alone, my meals were brief. I'd grab a handful of walnuts with some yogurt while looking at my phone.

I walked into the meeting room with my covered roasting pan, still hot, and still wearing my cooking apron. The tables were covered with pizza, chocolate chip cookies, pistachio fluff, Chinese food, cakes, chili, and cheese and crackers.

As we closed the last meeting, one woman said, "You are all welcome in my home."

Another woman thanked us for our courage as she handed out small heart-shaped charms with our names engraved on them.

As we said our husband's names aloud one last time, the names I now knew by heart, I felt grateful to have been part of this group with these seven women and Terri.

I had found a place to be and was ready to move on.

CHAPTER SEVENTY-NINE

Fun with Numbers

THE OFFER ON OUR house arrived on Mark's birthday, Thursday, April 23. After some negotiations, the buyer, my agent, and I agreed on a selling price the day of Mark's memorial birthday party, Sunday, April 26. The requested closing date was set for one day before my birthday, Friday, June 5. These significant dates happened out of my control. Was it just another coincidence, or was it Mark, who felt just a breath away, keeping his hand in things to protect or amuse me?

A girlfriend said to me, "Mark couldn't be here to buy you a piece of jewelry for your birthday this year, so he got your house sold for you!"

Our family held Mark's memorial birthday party at his favorite burger place in Raleigh. We invited family and friends to fill the place and celebrate Mark's birthday. His photo was placed by the cash registers and on the tables. The restaurant agreed to donate a percentage of the sales that day to Mayo Clinic MSA research. I loved overhearing people reminiscing and laughing, telling fun and sweet stories about Mark. It was a home-run afternoon. I was high as a kite. Mark would have loved it.

CHAPTER EIGHTY

Ceremony

IN THE SPRING, I went to the "Time of Remembrance and Renewal" event for families at hospice. Like the winter memorial event, it included inspirational readings and music. The theme was dragonflies.

The memorial began with the lighting of three candles. One represented each of us there that day, the second represented our beloved one who died, and the third represented hope for our journey into the future.

The woman conducting the service asked us to close our eyes and remember the gift our beloved gave us and how we can now share that gift in our lives. I remembered laughter. The ceremony ended with a procession to the front table. Each person selected a piece of sea glass or a bead to place inside a drawing of a dragonfly. I selected one bright orange piece of sea glass. We each said the deceased person's name into a microphone. There was something deeply touching about hearing each individual name spoken through the broken voices and tears.

At the end, when all the pieces of glass filled the dragonfly, it turned into a colorful and shimmering mosaic. A mosaic is a tender type of handiwork. It is a collection of broken pieces arranged to create a beautiful image. Each broken piece of glass represented a loved one. It was easy for me to spot the bright orange piece in the middle of one of the dragonfly's wings.

Then the host asked the children to come to the front. She had something special for them to do. A pair of ten-year-old twins, a boy about fourteen, another around eight, and a precious three-year-old girl, one hand playing with her braids, walked up toward her.

"To add to the beauty, the mosaic needs magic pixie dust. When you sprinkle the pixie dust, the mosaic becomes more beautiful and meaningful," the counselor said. Each child picked up a handful of sparkling dust and spread it across the mosaic. The mosaic was eventually hung near last year's butterfly mosaic in the waiting room of the grief center.

Since Mark's funeral and the triathlon, dragonflies have appeared in front of me in a persistent way—in paintings, books, places I'm visiting, on friends' jewelry, and buzzing around me on walks. Dragonflies have become a metaphor for me of life after death and Mark's continued presence in my life. Author Lyn Ragan wrote, "If we see a green dragonfly and we're open to receiving a message from our loved one, we can conclude a loved one is sending us a hug filled with love."[19]

Later, while I was visiting the cemetery with my cousins Curtis, Laurie, and Jeannie, and niece, Rebecca, a green dragonfly whizzed by Mark's headstone. We all noticed. As I explained what the dragonfly signified to me, it returned and landed on my shoulder. Jeannie found her phone and, with shaking hands, snapped a photo.

---

19   Lyn Ragan, *Signs from the Afterlife: Identifying Gifts from the Other Side* (Lyn Ragan: 2014), https://www.lynragan.com.

CHAPTER EIGHTY-ONE

A New Feeling

DAVID WAS MOVING TO DC. After being hired by a technology company called Tableau, he gave his two-week notice and left IBM. He had been living at home since shortly before Mark's passing. David and I had been terrific roommates. We enjoyed each other's company, often taking walks and having meals together. It was a comfort knowing he was near. Now it was time for him to spread his wings, and I was thrilled for him.

He rented a U-Haul truck and filled it with his belongings. I joined him for the drive to DC. We ate dinner in DC that night, and I hopped on a plane back to Raleigh the next morning.

My seat was in the last row. A man sat next to me. After the plane took off, I asked him a couple of questions. He was traveling to Raleigh for business and lived in a small town in Virginia.

He was about my age and wore blue jeans and light brown boots. He had on a long-sleeve plaid shirt of soft corduroy. The plaid was made up of several shades of blue. I studied the shirt. I wanted to touch the fabric. I even imagined his arm around me, the fabric feeling soft around my shoulders and against my cheek. I even pictured my head falling on his chest.

I noticed his hands as he opened his glasses case; his straight nose, white teeth, and brown eyes. I looked at his profile and observed which article he read from the magazine he was reading.

My sense of intimacy with this man rose as the plane flew across the sky. The plane descended thirty-five minutes later. He and I waited as the rows of passengers got up and shuffled down the aisle before we stood up. We smiled briefly at one another before exiting the plane and stood next to each other waiting for our luggage to arrive.

After grabbing our respective bags, we were out of each other's sight in seconds.

The invisible barrier between me and other men was gone. I could gaze at another man and not feel I had committed adultery. It was a first step.

CHAPTER EIGHTY-TWO

Dating?

I FELT AS ALONE as alone can be. I was missing Mark and the intimacy of a relationship. I missed the holding, laughter, and talking. If I lived another twenty or thirty years, that's a lot of years to be alone. I have love to give and want to remain soft and supple. If I'm not giving love, I feel stuck inside myself and worry I could turn hard. Mark and I talked frequently about my life after his death. His wish was for me to find someone to love.

I found a book at the library called *The Widow's Guide to Sex & Dating* and checked it out. My mood had changed from grim to lighthearted! It wasn't a "how-to." It was a witty fictional story full of engaging characters. The main character was widowed after a freak accident. The novel focused on her willingness to find herself and find a life after her husband's sudden death.

I never imagined dating and being with another man. I was beginning to understand that the next relationship would be different. No one can be Mark. Some things would be new. Maybe the man I found wouldn't have a sense of humor and wouldn't laugh as much. Maybe I would get introduced to the world of fly fishing—who knew? Whatever it would be, I was gearing up.

Over the next couple of weeks, I spoke with each of my kids privately. I wanted to know if they would be okay with me dating. They each responded similarly: they threw their heads back and laughed and said, "Of course." They preferred seeing me with someone rather than worrying about me being alone.

CHAPTER EIGHTY-THREE

Dearest Mark,

MY TIME IN OUR home is winding down. In ten days, I will move out of our home of nineteen years.

I often lie on the floor in our sitting area where your hospital bed was. Before your illness, this room held only a bookcase and a desk no one used. It was a room barely touched. Now, it's a room filled with the most significant memories.

This is where you lay for weeks before dying, where we'd circle you for hours, bringing the babies to you and placing them on your lap or nestling them onto your chest. You would watch us come and go, not speaking, but occasionally you'd smile or wink. The last few days of your life, you'd look up toward the corners of the room. It seemed like you saw something. I wish now I had asked what you were seeing.

I think of you, ache for you, and miss you. I remember your final weeks, days, hours, and minutes. I remember your face the night before you died. Your face shined and your eyes sparkled as you lovingly rested your gaze on each of us. You were taking one last look, as if you wanted to carry us with you, forever.

Were you telling us "I love you, thank you, I'll miss you, you're beautiful"? It seemed as though you were.

I didn't detect anger or bitterness, just acceptance and awareness of exactly what was happening.

I'm grateful for this sitting room. This house. But now it's time to move on.

I love you,

Julia

CHAPTER EIGHTY-FOUR

Sold!

DURING THE FINAL STAGES of the sale of our home, I missed Mark terribly and I wondered how he would have advised me during the grueling process. I felt picked to the bone by the buyers who asked for everything and got it. They were particularly insistent I pay for a new roof. It was the twenty-fifth year of a thirty-year roof. They sent me long emails and dozens of satellite photos of my roof. Negotiating didn't work; they wanted me to pay for a brand-new roof.

I was frustrated that the buyers brought this up at the very end of the due diligence period. At my wits' end, I bit the bullet and agreed to pay the full price of a new roof. It had been a game of chicken, and I blinked.

I wondered if Mark would have agreed to pay for a new roof. Would he have stopped bargaining with these people and moved on to another buyer? I was so unsure about what I was doing. It was a horrible experience.

A few days later, I was on my way to my realtor's office to sign the documents and end the due diligence period. I placed one of Mark's "Fuck You" T-shirts on the passenger seat beside me in the car. I needed him close. It was a reminder to laugh and feel his presence. Our friend Jonathan met me at the signing. It was a true act of support and friendship. For a brief moment, I imagined Mark at the meeting, sitting with me at the table, smiling at me. I smiled a tiny bit then turned my attention to the agents and documents. I didn't want to appear loony, looking out into space smiling. Signing the documents was bittersweet. There were two lines for two signatures. The world is made for couples. I pictured Mark's signature on one of them. I'm certain Mark would have been proud of me. I could hear him say, "You go, girl—you did it!"

A few months later, I found out from a neighbor that the house had been flooded after a botched roof renovation. I decided to drive by and see it. On my old front lawn were huge piles of debris, rolls of carpet, window screen, drywall, and roof parts. I counted at least a dozen work-men scrambling along the roof and around the house hauling debris and making repairs. Trucks lined the driveway and street.

Karma is a bitch!

SUMMER 2015:
MOVING FORWARD ON MY OWN

CHAPTER EIGHTY-FIVE

Nurturing

JENN'S PARENTS, ARLENE AND Michael, invited me over for dinner in early June. Along with Jeremy, Jenn, and Noah, we enjoyed a delicious meal inside their screened-in porch. We delighted in Noah's cute ways as he sat in his highchair. If he clapped, we clapped. If he laughed, we laughed.

After the meal ended, to my surprise, Arlene brought out a birthday cake with two tall silver candles. Michael and I have birthdays two days apart. Arlene handed me a gift along with one of her handmade 3-D cards. The card opened like a present; it was filled with delicate butterflies and a peacock feather. Inside the box, wrapped in green tissue, was a sparkly pin. This put me right over. My tears turned into audible sobs.

"So beautiful," I said through the tears.

I later reflected on the intense response. This past year had been one of taking care of myself 100 percent alone. I asked for help only when I was *truly* at the end of my rope. I was overly careful. I didn't want to over-ask.

When the beautiful cake with the silver candles and the sparkly gift appeared, I felt nurtured and cared for by others. It had been a long time since I had felt that way.

CHAPTER EIGHTY-SIX

Repair and Rejuvenate

NAOMI AND I SPOKE frequently about coping with the loss of a loved one after an extended illness. One night, before Mark died, we spoke about my eventual feelings after Mark's life ends.

"Think about how a fragile item is packed for shipping," she said. "There are layers of packing material to cushion the jostling of the delicate object against hard surfaces.

"After Mark dies, you won't be thinking clearly, and you'll need to imagine soft layers of cotton balls surrounding you to absorb the shocks and jolts of grief. The cocoon will be like a protective shield against overwhelming sadness and overly frayed nerves."

Eleven months after Mark died, I had planned back-to-back beach trips over twelve days in the middle of June. The first four days were with my children and two grandsons at Sunset Beach and coincided with my birthday. Since Mark's passing, I felt anxious prior to any holiday or birthday. It was difficult to celebrate without Mark. I noticed my usual anxiousness was gone at the beach. With my immediate family encircling me, it was as if my life was buffered by soft cotton balls. My nerves felt well cushioned. Noah, at twenty-one months, and Max, at seventeen months, were starting to interact, laugh, and connect. It was such a treat to see them play together!

At Sunset Beach, 2015.

The days with my family were filled with the usual beach activities: bicycling, building sand castles, strolling on the shore, eating meals. My birthday arrived. A lovely meal was prepared. We sat on the back deck under a clear sky with gentle breezes. After dessert, Emily called everyone into the living room and handed me an eggplant-colored nylon tote bag decorated with curled gold ribbon.

I found a card that left me almost speechless. Each of my children acknowledged the challenges I had faced, the strength I showed, and their bright hope for my future.

"I hope I haven't been a burden," I said. They all shook their heads.

I reached into the bag and pulled out two watercolor pads of paper, watercolor paints, and brushes. I held all the art supplies in my hands.

How perfect. Nothing else could have been more meaningful. I hadn't lifted a brush or painted anything in three years.

"To be used in Beaufort," they chorused.

After the weekend with my kids, I headed north to stay by myself for five days at a friend's beach house in Beaufort. I planned to renew, reflect, and move on. I switched gears from family time to alone time.

Each day, I selected a different location around the beach house to paint. I sat on the back deck overlooking the sound and painted the water, marsh, dock, and sky. I found a spot in the shade in the front and painted trees. Another day, I painted flowers in the garden by the side garage. At night, I painted inside the house. I dabbed the brushes into the containers of paint and water then onto the paper, letting the brush guide my hand. Abstract shapes and colors emerged.

In the middle of the week, the sale of my house was completed. The sale was a huge milestone for me. I drove into Beaufort's historic downtown to be around other people and collect my thoughts. While I was walking, I spotted a sparkly lemon-yellow visor in a store window. I went into the store and bought it to wear—a celebratory hat. I had them cut off the tags so I could wear it right away. I took a few selfies in my new hat.

I was getting hungry and treated myself to crab cakes. Wearing my new sunshine-yellow hat while eating crab cakes made me feel happy. It was my first time celebrating anything alone, particularly something as humongous as selling a home.

House sold. I was now done with that part of my life.

The next evening, I strolled the boardwalk. I looked out at the river and listened to live music. Occasionally I sat on a bench and people-watched. As I leaned against the railing gazing at the sparkling water and boats sailing by, a middle-aged man approached me. He asked my name. I answered, Julia. I asked what his name was. He said Robert.

"Isn't there an actress named Julia Roberts?" he joked.

Ba-da-boom! I thought to myself and faked a smile.

He asked where I was from. I answered Raleigh. I repeated the same question of him. He answered Swansboro. He asked what I did. I didn't want to answer; suddenly it felt like he knew too much about me.

"I do this and that," I said in a light tone of voice.

He was looking at my ringless finger.

"I'm about to go on the sunset cruise; it's just an hour and a half. I'd like to treat you, as my guest. Would you like to join me, and you can do 'this and that' on the boat?"

"Oh, no thank you," I replied with a little laugh.

"How about joining me for dinner after the cruise, when I return?" he asked.

"Oh, thanks, but no thank you. I'm meeting friends." We both knew I was lying.

I thanked him again, shook his hand, and turned and walked away down the boardwalk. *Whoa, whoa,* I thought.

If he had been more my type, would I have said yes to his invitation?

I returned to the town center and sat on one of the benches. I was lost in thought when another man gently grabbed my shoulder and asked, "What are you thinking about?" I turned my head in his direction. He continued talking in a flirtatious manner. We spoke for ten minutes or so before I went to my car and hurried back to the beach house. Two men approaching me out of the blue was enough for one evening!

The last night in Beaufort took a frightening turn. It was late, and I was in the upstairs guest bedroom reading. Gradually I began to feel nauseated, achy, and chilled. I threw up a couple of times. I huddled under the covers, but the symptoms didn't go away. They increased.

As the evening wore on, I was getting more ill and weak. I was in a somewhat isolated beach house. The one or two houses near me were vacant. I felt too weak and frightened to drive. I had no idea where the nearest hospital or urgent care was. My kids were more than three hours away in Raleigh.

I worried about falling asleep. I believed I might die alone in a bed in Beaufort. I believed if I didn't get seen by a doctor, my symptoms might spiral out of control; I'd fall asleep and not wake up. I became anxious and teary and had trouble breathing.

I called Naomi. She couldn't do anything for me, but she had a way of comforting me. I relaxed a bit after our phone conversation. I began to believe her assurances that nothing was going to happen, that I'd be fine. I was delighted when I awoke the next morning. I was alive! My discomfort appeared to have been food poisoning.

After four nights in Sunset Beach with my family and five days alone in Beaufort, it was time to continue to the next and last part of my beach vacation.

My book club gathers yearly for a weekend in Emerald Isle. Each year, we establish a theme accompanied by talking, walking, eating, drinking, and games. Sometimes we've danced, made crafts, done yoga, and even kayaked.

This year's game was Cards Against Humanity and the drink was Moscow mules, and a terrific shrimp boil was thrown on sheets of brown paper across the dining table.

The art project was making princess headbands. We gave ourselves princess names. There were Princess Winter-Spring-Summer-Fall, Princess Emerald Eyes, Princess Good Vibrations, and Princess Go with the Flow, to name a few. I was Princess Bubbie-licious!

After dinner and craft-making, we sat around a firepit making s'mores and singing songs from musicals, '60s folk songs, the Beatles, and the Beach Boys.

It was heaven.

The next day when we were sitting around the dining table eating lunch, I was talking with the person sitting next to me. A split second later, I *had* to leave. I quietly stood up and, without saying a word to anyone, headed out the door. I walked across the road to the beach and began heading north, walking in my bare feet along the water's edge.

I walked toward a group of young adults standing in a circle about ankle deep in the water. They caught my eye. I watched them intently. Slowly, the slenderest of the men, in red swim trunks, turned and looked piercingly into my eyes. I slowed my steps and maintained eye contact with him until I walked past. I sped up. I looked back, and he was fully engaged with his group.

I could not get his eyes out of my mind as I walked another twenty minutes. When I turned around, the group was still there at the shoreline. The man in the red swim trunks was in the exact spot where he and I made eye contact. His body language was completely different: more hang-loose like his buddies. He didn't turn to look at me. His eyes and my encounter with him stayed with me the rest of the day and night.

Call me imaginative, but here's what I concluded: I left my friends suddenly and *had* to walk to the beach alone. I approached a man and had an intense and unexpected encounter with him. He was *seeing* me, not glancing at me. He *knew* me. Had Mark's soul entered that man for the briefest moment to look at me? Was I meeting Mark eye to eye, which is what I yearned for since he died?

It reminded me of another moment, a few months earlier while seated at a restaurant. A waiter approached our table from behind me and placed his hand briefly on my shoulder. A hot electric jolt surged through my entire body. It was startling, unusually intimate, and *couldn't be ignored*. It was like nothing I had felt before from a casual tap on a shoulder. Was it Mark? I thought about the waiter's touch and the eyes of the man on the beach. I've looked into thousands of eyes and been casually touched thousands of times. Both moments were different and became etched in my mind. I'm grounded in reality, but touches of magic enter my world.

I was grateful to drive back to Raleigh alone after twelve days at the beach.

It was the end of June 2015. Mark had been gone almost a year. I looked back at the time and knew I honored him in every way. He deserved every tribute. The tributes filled me with beautiful memories and were another way to connect with him. I didn't just go through the motions.

In Mark's honor, I lit a memorial candle during every holiday, including Halloween and Father's Day. I attended the memorial events that hospice offered in winter and spring. I placed a nameplate for Mark in our temple's sanctuary, celebrated his birthday at his favorite burger place in Raleigh surrounded by family and friends, joined a support group, and talked regularly to a therapist. I sold our home and bought a home. I paid my bills and taxes on time. I traveled alone and with family and friends. I took finance classes and even shot a pistol for the first time.

I hadn't sat still all year. I was busy moving to stay afloat—like in water ballet, if you stop, you drown. I didn't want to drown that first year.

Life isn't simple or predictable. I longed for the blessed routine. It's hard to find. Life is upheaval and chaos, followed by calm and sweetness and returning to upheaval and chaos. That is the routine, and maybe it is blessed.

CHAPTER EIGHTY-SEVEN

The Treasure Map

JEREMY ASKED ME TO get the Treasure Map, aka the Road Map.

Mark began writing the Road Map soon after his diagnosis in September 2011. It was a twenty-six-page document with all pertinent financial information. This included bank account numbers; life, auto, health, dental, home, and umbrella insurance policy information; passwords, user names, websites; and contact information for our attorney, CPA, financial adviser, and insurance agents.

There was information on where to find last year's tax returns and our wills and trust. There was an entire page devoted to monthly bills. He explained the purpose of the bill and whether it's paid monthly, quarterly, every six months, or yearly. He included the numbers for the pest control, cable, telephone, and HVAC companies, and the lawn service. Helpful household details included when to change the water filter in the refrigerator and how often the roof gutters need to be cleaned. There was information on how to care for my car and how to prepare for taxes.

Mark included a comment section in a column next to all accounts. This is where he explained the account and offered possible answers to any questions I might have. He listed the person to contact regarding each account. In one comment section, he gave clear directions about the age I should begin Medicare.

The page that filled me with a particular type of sadness was the one explaining his business bank account. Under comments he wrote, "This is the business account. Westwood Executive Search Group is now out of business. This checking account was closed as of 8/15/12. There is nothing further regarding this account."

There was something brave about his words. Not a hint of self-pity.

Listed on another page was what to do after he dies. How many death certificates I would need, when to contact the Social Security office, the process of filing claims for the life insurance policies, and a "no embalming" request.

There was a full page of bullet points. A few examples:

- Whatever you don't understand, it's okay. You have plenty of people to ask for help.

- I wish I wasn't dead.

- Good Luck and Have Fun.

He updated the document every three to four months over a two-and-a-half-year period. After an update, he'd print it out, staple it, and with a bit of a smile and serious eyes, hand it to me to place somewhere for safekeeping. I understood what it was, but I never read it. I was afraid and overwhelmed with having to know all this information. I'd take it from his hands and slip it into the bottom of a drawer. He never pressed me to read it. He figured it would be there when I was ready, at a critical time when information was needed.

Before my house went on the market, I placed the Treasure Map in my safe deposit box at the bank. One day, after Mark had passed away, Jeremy needed a password from the document and asked me to retrieve it. I went to the bank and brought the safe deposit box into a small, enclosed room with a chair and table.

I found the document buried at the bottom of the box. I pulled it out, carefully placing it on the table in front of me, and decided to read it for the first time. I read it slowly, in its entirety.

What I discovered was a twenty-six-page love letter. Like Mark, it was not flowery or sentimental. It was practical. It was for me. His precious care of me. His heart was in that document. I felt him on every page as I read each word, dash, and digit.

Mark was the real treasure. A treasure who never boasted, insisted, or pressed anything on me. He was a mound of goodness and love.

CHAPTER EIGHTY-EIGHT

Unveiling Ceremony

THE FIRST ANNIVERSARY OF Mark's death, or *yahrzeit*, was approaching. I was in the midst of planning the unveiling ceremony. I had never been to an unveiling ceremony before. All I knew is that I wanted it to be the opposite of Mark's funeral. It would be intimate. In attendance would be my five children, Richard, Sarah, Doe, and me.

The nine of us would gather at the cemetery around the newly placed headstone. It would be veiled ahead of time by the stonemason who carved, delivered, and placed the headstone where Mark was buried. I imagined the veil decreasing the initial shock of seeing Mark's name on a headstone.

I wanted the unveiling ceremony to have meaning: something more than just showing up. The focus of our attention would be on Mark, our relationship to him, and how it's changed after a year since his passing. We would confront our loss. It would be a day to bring all of us together. I asked for input from my kids. Our ceremony evolved over several weeks. I worked closely with Emily; she created the booklets and helped assign the readings of the prayers and poems to family members.

During the last weekend in June, I went to a dinner party. I visited with a woman I hadn't seen in a long time. She had recently attended an unveiling of the headstone of her friend in New York.

I gravitate toward ritual and listened intently as she described the custom of writing letters to the deceased and reading them at the unveiling ceremony. She said the letters were read out loud just above a whisper. Whispering was more tender than saying the words in your head. Once the letters are read, the reader rips them into five pieces and burns them. I returned home that night and wrote a long letter to Mark.

I told my children, Richard, Sarah, and Doe that I had written a letter and planned on reading it at the ceremony. They were welcome to do so if they wished. They all decided to write letters to Mark.

A week or so later, I met with my grief counselor, Maureen. I described the unveiling ceremony to her. I just wasn't sure where to burn the letters; the cemetery didn't have a designated place for burning paper.

Her eyes lit up as she reminded me of the Cosmic Post directly outside the grief center. It has a metal container for items to be burned. There is a small drawer underneath the container for lighting. As the papers burn, smoke and ash are released into the sky. Kismet!

I would be able to send all our messages to Mark through smoke signals! Ashes to ashes and dust to dust.

CHAPTER EIGHTY-NINE

July 16, 2015

WHAT A NIGHT. IT was ten days before Mark's first yahrzeit, and his presence filled the night in my dreams!

The first dream was simple:

Mark got into bed with me, the bed I'm sleeping in at Jeremy and Jenn's house. He was wearing an indigo blue long-sleeved shirt. I noticed the back of him first. He turned over and spent a few minutes getting himself comfortable under the covers. He looked healthy. I was wonderstruck. His eyes opened, and for a fleeting moment we looked into each other's eyes; he touched me near my belly button.

I woke up and couldn't return to sleep for forty-five minutes.

After I fell back asleep, Mark returned in another dream:

He was standing in a room wearing a white T-shirt. He was talking to Jeremy and me. I turned to Jeremy and said, "Do you see him?"

"Yes," Jeremy answered.

The three of us continued talking while we moved through several rooms of a house. Mark stood holding a baby. Jeremy was lying on a bed. Mark suddenly became weak and gently fell on the bed near Jeremy. He looked away and said, "I'm missing something."

"No you're not, stay here!" I said desperately.

Mark's face changed shape and color, turning pale, then green. His mouth became a square. He looked at me with an unusual faraway expression.

I woke up screaming.

I stayed up at least an hour and then fell asleep again.

The next dream:

I am on a train to see Mark. I read in the paper there is an event at a hospital. They are bringing Mark and others there for some kind of celebration. My eyes are filled with sleep. It is difficult to see where I am going. I get off at the wrong train stop in the wrong city.

I get back on the train and exit at the next stop and walk to the place. A woman greets me. I tell her I am there to see Mark; this is the day he would be brought out.

She answers yes, this is the day. We walk down the corridors. The floors and walls are sticky. My eyes are still full of sleep, I splash water on my face in order to see better. I keep imagining seeing Mark and am excited.

We keep walking down the darkening corridor. I realize I am not going to see him; he is not there. He died last year.

I woke up crying and disoriented.

CHAPTER NINETY

July 17, 2015

THE NIGHT OF EMILY'S birthday, I dreamt of Mark again.

I'm in a small bedroom with Jeremy and Mark. Mark is wearing an indigo blue shirt again. Jeremy sits on the bed with tears in his eyes as he looks at his dad. The three of us chat. Mark sits right next to me on the bed; our thighs touch.

"Have you seen Emily this year?" I ask, turning to him.

Mark raises three fingers and says softly and earnestly, "Three times."

These dreams had a different quality than others I have had. They were very sensory and vivid. I felt visited by Mark.

Mark's indigo shirt was particularly vivid. I Googled indigo, a color between blue and violet that has multiple meanings. It is the color of the night sky. It can be associated with depth, mystery, wisdom, and spirituality. Indigo is tranquil and calm. In Hinduism, indigo is the bridge between heaven and earth and between life and death.

CHAPTER NINETY-ONE

July 19, 2015

AS I HEADED CLOSER to Mark's first yahrzeit, the days felt slower, and I was reflective. Mark had passed on, moved over to someplace else. We were on opposite sides of what, I don't know. Mark was squarely present in my consciousness. I ached for him every day.

I was eager to be at his gravesite and read my letter to him.

I looked behind me and saw a year of growth, reflection, and reorientation to the world. I looked ahead to the immediate future and was excited to move into my new home.

CHAPTER NINETY-TWO

July 24, 2015

THE CLOSING ON MY house went smoothly. My realtor, Carole, was with me. It was uneventful. I felt relaxed. Afterward, we celebrated at a nearby restaurant. She gave me gifts for my new home: cocktail napkins with my initials in gold lettering and address labels. There was my name, solo, in a beautiful font above my new address.

CHAPTER NINETY-THREE

July 26, 2015: The Unveiling

RICHARD, SARAH, DOE, JEREMY, Jenn, Emily, James, David, and I met at the cemetery at ten in the morning. We gathered around the veiled headstone under a sunny sky. I reached down and gently removed the white cotton veil. We all needed a few moments to take in the sight.

Mark's headstone.

The children and I had created the inscription for his marker in the spring. It took us several weeks to find the right words. My only advice to them was, choose carefully. These words will literally be etched in stone; they cannot be deleted later. There was so much to say about him; we went through several versions. I jokingly said we should add, "Read his book!"

Our family's narrative included life with a chronically and terminally ill dad and husband. This became part of our personal and family journey. We have our scars and our strengths from the sorrow we felt. The tragedy of Mark's illness broke parts of each of us. We found ourselves in our new broken pieces. And, within our broken pieces, we found Mark.

The words we chose to honor Mark on his tombstone were perfect: *A life full of love, laughter and courage. He lives on through all who knew him.*

Emily handed out the booklets filled with poems and prayers. The early writers of prayers were poets and spiritual mystics. The words we chose were filled with love, hope, fear, and wishes and words of comfort, healing, joy, and connection.

We each had a part to read. Jeremy began with Psalm 23. The images are clear and comforting in this prayer. "He makes me lie down in green pastures, he leads me beside quiet waters." Mark is lying in a green meadow. We pass gentle streams and lakes during the drive to the cemetery. "Though I walk through the valley of the shadow of death, I will fear no evil, for you are with me; your rod and your staff, they comfort me." Mark walked through a sorrowful disease; he didn't let it harm his soul. No matter the pain of MSA, Mark transcended his grief with love and hope. "Surely goodness and love will follow me all the days of my life."

Doe was next. She read a short poem.

Jenn led the Kel Maleh Rachamim. It is always read at an unveiling ceremony. This prayer is a plea. The hope is for the Divine Presence to shelter Mark's soul "with the cover of his wings forever and bind his soul in the bond of life." Another clear message of protection, remembering, and loving Mark. We laughed as Jenn struggled through the Hebrew (we later agreed Mark would appreciate the humor!). James read the English translation.

Then we individually read our letters to Mark. Jenn had brought a blanket, and we laid it on the ground by Mark's headstone.

I read first. Everyone else stepped away, twelve feet or so, near the trees, to give the reader privacy.

I sat down on my knees and bent way over. I touched and rubbed Mark's headstone while I read my entire letter, just above a whisper, crying all the way through.

I'm here at your gravesite with our children, Richard, Sarah, and your mom. We're together, the way you wanted us to be. I recently understood what you were trying to tell us the night before you died. Your hands with fingertips touching, your eyes fiercely looking into mine: you were telling the family to stay together. And we have.

I'm here to find a way to connect with you. I want to find you here, near me, near us. Are you here? I've had a complicated year—full of changes, challenges, decisions, and yearnings. I have longed for your presence so often it brings tears to my eyes thinking how frequently I wished for you. I tried bargaining with whoever, to have you for an hour, then pleading for fifteen minutes, or finally asking for two minutes. Just to have you look into my eyes. No one looks into my eyes the way you did. What I'd do to hold your hand, hear your voice and laugh.

I have not been touched in years; it's painful to not be touched.

I'm here to touch the spot where your body rests. To remember you, to remember us.

I have had hundreds of questions for you. I reached out to others like you advised.

I felt vulnerable in a new way.

I felt alone in a new way.

I felt out of sorts and off-kilter in a new way.

I felt strong in a new way.

I have had to adjust to new relationships, expand some, and contract others. I miss you terribly. I miss the relationship you would have had with Noah and Max. They are full of fun and moxie, totally adorable! They would have LOVED you so much!! I show them your photograph. Noah recognizes you and says, "Grandpa Mark." Max will soon say your name too.

I want to know how you're doing. Are you present in my life? Or are you happy in some awesome and dazzling place? Or are you simply gone . . . no more. Am I speaking to the wind? I've seen signs pointing to your presence, and I wonder.

I'm starstruck by our children, and you would be too. You would be incredibly proud of Jeremy and Jenn, Emily and James, and David. They are living their lives in beautiful ways. Each of them are sources of comfort and friendship to me.

I would have loved sharing this beautiful time with you—cherishing our children and grandchildren together. I miss sharing these experiences with you! You'd have Noah and Max laughing with your funny faces, silly games, and stories. Games and stories only you would come up with.

I cannot believe you're not here. Are you going to walk over to me right now from behind those trees?!

You've been gone a long time. I'll take you back if it would be possible for you to return.

I'll take you.

I stood next to Mark's mother as she read her letter and smiled as she added a P.S. and P.S.S. After she read, I walked toward the trees where everyone stood in a semicircle. One by one, each person walked up to the blanket, sat in various ways, and quietly read aloud their letter, just above a whisper. I could tell their hearts were pouring out to Mark. At one point, a dragonfly flew among us. Emily, Jenn, and I caught each other's eyes and smiled.

After the readings were completed, I asked everyone to tear their letters into five pieces and place the pieces in the white bag I held open. I looked into the bag at the torn papers. There was the wholeness of us. Now, shredded and broken.

We reopened our booklets and completed the ceremony. David read a poem. Emily read the Mourner's Kaddish in Hebrew. It does not mention death; life is being blessed in this prayer. Richard and Sarah read the translation in English together. I closed our service with a poem.

I opened some purple tissue filled with stones and shells collected for Mark's unveiling. In Judaism, placing stones at a gravesite symbolizes remembrance. They don't wilt like flowers. They are strong and solid. Everyone selected a few and placed them on Mark's headstone. His headstone was covered in love.

July 27, 2015

CAROLE WAS WITH ME when I picked up the keys to my new home. She joined me as I drove up and parked in my new driveway, unlocked the door, and walked in.

PART

IX

FINDING MEANING

The Afterlife Conference

We are not human beings having a spiritual experience.
We are spiritual beings having a human experience.
—PIERRE TEILHARD DE CHARDIN

WHEN MARK WAS ALIVE, though in failing health, I experienced hearing Mark's voice when I wasn't with him. It was an auditory hallucination. It also happened after he passed away. There are the five senses, and I had to acknowledge the unexplained sixth sense. I felt and saw Mark in various places, through others, and in my dreams.

Before the yahrzeit, I visited a medium in Durham. It was the ultimate act of desperation and something I had never imagined doing. By going to a medium, I was begging someone to bring Mark to me. After turning her head to the side and blinking a few times, she had answers, straight from Mark! I fell hook, line, and sinker. I wasn't as prepared as I should have been before showing up to her home office, because when she asked me, "What questions do you have for Mark?" all I could come up with was, "Are you in pain?" And that made me cry.

She snapped her fingers and answered, "He's not in any pain, he's not in his body, he doesn't need his body anymore." I spent an hour with her. I had been searching for Mark for over a year. She allowed me to place

Mark in the room with us. He was seeing me. He knew how our children and grandchildren were doing. He was watching us. While I was with her, I believed her. It was a dream come true.

In May 2016, I attended a conference in St. Louis called "The Science and Spirit of Death, Grief, and Beyond." I went with a good friend who was battling cancer. I was wide open to the experience and eager for a fresh viewpoint. Before the conference was to begin, I received an email from the medium I was scheduled to see: "Hello, soon-to-be Spiritual Astronauts!" How can you not love that kind of welcome!?

The night before I flew to the conference, I had a dream. I was in a large, sterile, gray room with a few other people. Dozens of dead people approached us. We had to clean them then return them to their burial spot. One of the dead men got angry, and I needed another person to help calm him. I said, "He's weak. It won't be too difficult to lay him back down." I didn't recognize anyone; Mark wasn't there.

The conference itself was like a dream; it validated my almost twelve-year journey with MSA and loss. At the start of Mark's illness, I often felt I was in the dark. I found my way with the use of ritual, community, dreams, creativity, celebration, and therapy. These concepts were the big themes of the conference. The workshops tapped into my five senses: sight, hearing, smell, taste, and touch. The conference pushed me to trust my sixth sense. The knowledge I gained was like a warm blanket, comforting and reassuring.

The attendees were like-minded individuals. Often in a workshop, I'd see tears in their eyes and smiles on their faces. I felt their yearning and vulnerability. We all wanted to connect with our DP (shorthand used at the conference for "dead person"). I felt safe at this conference.

One day, I met a woman in her midseventies during lunch. Her husband had died fifteen years earlier. She communicated with him every day. And she wanted to let me in on a little secret: her husband has met Steve Jobs on the other side! The two of them were working on a phone that will connect the living with the nonliving. She was expecting her first phone call by the end of summer. She was giddy with excitement. On one hand, it sounded silly. On the other hand, it was endearing. I could understand her deepest desire to connect with her husband and hear his voice.

I met another woman whose mother had died fifty years earlier. She came to the conference to mark the anniversary and finally let go of her anger. She was there to find peace in her life.

The speakers were hospice physicians, shamanic healers, chaplains certified in death, psychologists, registered nurses, grief yogis, and near-death experiencers.

One of the workshops I attended was "Grief as a Mystical Journey." At one point, we were asked to draw while listening to music. I closed my eyes. As soon as the pen touched the paper, tears filled my eyes and poured down my face. I drew, letting my hand and arm become one. I didn't guide my arm; it moved separate from me, pressing harder on the left side of the paper. The pen moved vigorously up, down, and in slender ovals. The pen barely touched the paper; the lines were light and delicate. Eyes closed, tears flowed. Dark to light, earth to spirit. I opened my eyes, and there within the ovals and thin and thick lines was Mark's face on the paper.

Several of the workshops began with a simple shamanistic ritual. The shaman whistled and shook a maraca. Standing, as a group we rotated clockwise, starting in the direction of east, then, south, west, north, then lowered down to touch the ground and Mother Earth, and raised our hands up high toward Father Sky. I joined in, thinking, *When in Rome . . .*

During another workshop I was guided into a "soul journey." Once again, I closed my eyes. I saw myself walking slowly toward a weeping willow tree. As I sat at the base of the tree, the trunk morphed into arms and embraced me. I saw my loneliness and was offered courage by the presence of my great-grandmother. She handed me a blue sapphire before departing.

I learned at the conference that there are death doulas and midwives. Perhaps it would have been helpful to have one with me to interpret what was unfolding the night Mark died. But being alone with him the moment he took his last breath has become a cherished memory.

I meticulously reconstructed the timeline of Mark's last living day. I needed to know as accurately as possible the moment his eyes closed for the last time. I concluded it was sometime between 4:00 and 4:15 p.m. on Saturday, July 26. What was his last view of our world? I was downstairs with Max, Tracy, and Leni. I wished he had been looking at me. Two years after he died, I was still feeling anguish and guilt. Even though I was next to him when he took his last breath later that night, I wanted us to be looking at each other when he closed his eyes. I wanted to be his last view of our world.

The night I returned home from the conference, I had a dream:

Mark is alive and in a reclined position in front of me. He isn't sitting on the furniture but floating in the air. A filmmaker stands next to me. The filmmaker is filming Mark, expecting him to say the lines in the script. Mark goes off script, looks at me and says, "I miss you." The filmmaker lowers his camera and stops filming.

Synchronicity

CARL JUNG WAS THE first to describe synchronicity: meaningful coincidence.

I have been on a spiritual journey since 2004 when Mark's first symptom appeared. My healing was rooted in finding myself. Everyone and everything that entered my life felt rich with purpose. Nothing has seemed casual or inconsequential.

I reflected on my close friendship with the terminally ill boy, who was also named Mark, living at Rancho Los Amigos Hospital, and the year I spent working with physically disabled individuals.

I remembered our friend in LA who suffered from MSA, an odd coincidence given the rarity of the disease. He was a few years older than Mark, with a wife and two children around our children's ages. Mark once joked with him: "How did we end up with the same disease; did we share a corned beef sandwich?"

He died five months after Mark.

Mark's diagnosis of MSA came during the most introspective time in the Jewish calendar, compounding our already intensive soul-searching. Our friends Roxanne and Dan live only an hour away from Mayo Clinic in Minnesota. It was wonderful having them with us to offer support each visit we made there.

The sea glass Emily and I spotted at hospice. Meeting Sandra, whose husband also suffered from MSA, at just the right time in Raleigh. At the last moment, a few days before Mark's passing, Richard changing his flight by one day, allowing him to see Mark one last time.

I saw dots and connected them. They formed a design of meaning and purpose, and this brought me comfort.

Since Mark's passing, there have been countless synchronistic moments. The two standouts are:

During Mark's illness, Lisa, an acquaintance of ours, came to our home every other week and led Mark in chair yoga. She shared Mark's love of music and incorporated his favorite tunes into the sessions. I didn't see her often after Mark's passing. Over the year, I followed her life on Facebook, noticing her husband's retirement and that he started painting. He was going to be displaying his paintings at a huge outdoor arts festival near downtown. It was a gorgeous day, so I decided to drive there. I'd see his paintings and, I hoped, chat with Lisa. I parked my car and walked toward the stately home where his paintings were set out. As I approached, I heard Jeremy's song "Waves" coming from the porch. Lisa was leaning on the railing. We saw each other at the same moment.

We ran toward one another and hugged.

"I can't believe you're here. I had decided to put on some music, and thought, I'm going to play Mark's playlist, I haven't heard it in a long time. I was listening to the first song, 'Waves,' and thinking, I wish someone who knew Mark would show up. And there you were, Julia, walking toward me!"

We kept looking into each other's eyes, laughing, smiling, tearing up, and saying how wild it was I'd show up at that exact moment.

During Mark's illness, our friends Marvin and Carla would occasionally come by with dinner. One night, Mark asked Carla if she'd like to drive with me and look at condos. A few weeks later, Carla and I drove around downtown while Mark and Marvin stayed behind and visited together.

At the same time I sold my home, Carla and Marvin were looking for a home to remodel. They put offers on two homes far away from where I bought mine. Both offers fell through.

After I moved into my new home, Carla visited and fell in love with it. She brought Marvin over, and he loved it too. By the end of the week, they had made an offer on the lot across the street.

The three of us were celebrating after their offer was accepted. Marvin turned to Carla and asked, "Should I tell her?"

Carla nodded. They both had tears in their eyes.

"Julia, remember when we came over to your house with dinner a few months before Mark passed away? While you and Carla went looking at condos, Mark told me he really hoped you'd move. I told him we were thinking of moving too. We wanted to find a midcentury ranch, a fixer-upper.

"'Perhaps you and Julia would be neighbors one day,' Mark said to me. That wasn't our initial plan, but here we are, living across the street from each other," Marvin said, smiling.

These meaningful coincidences were my way of seeing beginnings, not endings.

CHAPTER NINETY-SEVEN

Hearts

I MOVED INTO MY new home. I unpacked, little by little. No rush. Life kept going.

There was the starkest contrast between Mark alive in my life and Mark gone out of my life. With Mark alive, my life was full of intimacy. There was an intricate weave between the two of us. As years were added to our life, the weave became more beautiful.

Being a widow isn't being one person after being part of a couple. I felt more like I was half a person after being part of a oneness. My home was quieter. The hardest sixty seconds of the day happened each time I entered my home alone. When the cable technician came to install my system, I stayed in the same room with him the whole time he was working just so I could be near another person.

I had to do something to change how I felt. I attended a happy hour for new residents. A few people asked me which man in the crowd was my husband. I didn't want people to feel sorry for me or uncomfortable that my husband had died, so I said with a smile: "I'm moving in solo."

I was surprised to discover I didn't want to create another garden of my own. I let the builder put in whatever plants were offered as an option.

In downsizing, I left many things behind. I took only those things I loved along with the ones that were part of our life together. The mandala tapestry Mark and I bought in Sausalito, that once hung in our dining room, became the focal point in my new living room. The delicate intertwined candlesticks from the Mayo Clinic gift store sit nearby on a shelf. Mark's book is next to my bed inside a drawer. Periodically, I reach for it, close my eyes, open to a random page, and place my finger somewhere. Opening my eyes, I read the paragraph. Like a horoscope, the message I receive is just what I need to hear from Mark.

Having made the leap safely from our life to my life, I now have fewer anxiety attacks. I no longer scream in my car. Although it wasn't easy, I managed to transition from connected couplehood to aloneness to loneliness, and then on to being just me.

When I fell in love with Mark and we got married, I did not know I would someday be living with a spouse with a terminal condition. I could not have imagined the challenges, conversations, and insights such a turn of events would bring to my life. I was not prepared for how significantly and beautifully all my relationships would change, particularly the one with myself.

I have new relationships, new projects and plans. I was redefining my life.

I celebrated my sixtieth birthday with a party at a nightclub in downtown Raleigh. I wanted to dance with family and friends surrounding me. The chaplain and others often said they were a witness to my pain. Now, family and friends could circle me and witness my rediscovered joy.

I packed up my brushes and joined my cousin Curtis for a four-day landscape painting workshop in Santa Fe.

This is my one and only life, and it will forever include losing Mark. I move forward, bringing along the paradoxes and the paintbrushes.

One day, Noah and I were visiting Grandma Doe. I was holding Noah in my arms. Doe stood next to us looking at a photo on the wall of her husband, Danny; Mark; and her sister, Betty. She raised her index finger and tapped each person in the photo, exclaiming, "Gone, gone, gone."

Noah, eighteen months at the time, threw his head back and laughed. He repeated, in his high-pitched baby voice, while stabbing the air with his index finger, "Gone, gone, gone!!" Doe and I burst out laughing. Mark would have laughed at this too!

If you ask Noah, "Where is Grandpa Mark?" he points to his tiny chest and says, "In my heart."

I know if Mark's soul is somewhere, we are all in his heart too.

Top row, left to right: Jeremy with Noah, David with Max, Elena (David's wife), and James. Bottom row, left to right: Doc, me, Emily with Maya, Jenn with Ellie, 2019.

Epilogue

I WROTE AND PERFORMED this story for The Monti on January 30, 2016. The video recording is available at www.themonti.org:

My husband died eighteen months ago. Before he died, he made certain things clear to me. First, he wanted me to sell our house. Second, as hard as it was for him to say, he wanted me to find a new relationship.

I couldn't imagine doing either. I told him I couldn't leave our home—that's where I had all my memories of our kids and him. And I could never imagine myself with another man.

He said there will be ghosts in this house, and he worried about me being alone. We had this discussion several times. We'd go back and forth. He'd shrug, smile, and end the discussion with "Do what you want. I won't be here."

Well, he was right. Shortly after he died, I wasn't comfortable living in our home alone. It felt hollow. I had trouble sleeping there. A few months later, I found a realtor, and the house went on the market. At the same time, I picked a lot in a new subdivision and started building a home from scratch.

My house sold in April, and I moved into my new home in July, exactly one year and one day after Mark's passing. It was the start of a new chapter in my life.

A few weeks later, I discovered a new feeling. I didn't recognize what it was at first, because I had never felt it before—loneliness.

My husband was right about that too. I had another challenge to solve.

With trepidation and excitement, I joined two online dating sites. The action happened right away. There were scams, oddballs, and an assortment of characters. There were also genuine people looking to connect.

I met my first date on a Sunday at the Nasher Museum at 2:00 p.m. We planned on meeting in the lobby. I arrived first. It felt surreal to be waiting for a man that wasn't my husband. I distracted myself by looking at the artwork on the wall.

Suddenly, a man's arms were around me; he stepped on my toe and sang the John Lennon song "Julia" in my ear. I pulled back to see him. I realized his profile photo was about ten years old.

I also knew in a blink of an eye: there was no future with him. But I realized it took courage on both our parts to dress up and meet a total stranger. So I pointed to nearby chairs and said, "Let's sit and talk."

We were together an hour. At one point, he excused himself to use the bathroom.

"Please don't leave while I'm gone," he said.

"Don't worry. I'll be here when you get back."

At that moment, I saw my husband's image appear sitting in a chair across from me. He was smiling at me and drawing a finger across his throat as if to say, "This isn't the guy."

"I know, I know," I responded.

I waited for the guy to return; we walked out of the museum together.

Hope springs eternal. I went back online and looked at profiles again. I was looking for my husband. This one looks like Mark, this guy looks like Mark. I'd read their profiles and they were nothing like Mark.

Mark was hysterically funny, full of love, and he made me feel safe.

Then I met Paul, a widower. He didn't look like Mark. He was kind. He was a happy person and surprisingly spry!

The relationship was slow moving, though we saw each other once a week, maybe twice. We texted once or twice a week. I was setting the pace. I was holding back. I was trying to form myself around a new man. At times, it felt artificial. I couldn't feel the chemistry. I struggled to create a couplehood. I couldn't get in sync.

He once asked me what I expected when I first met him. I answered I had no expectations, just to have fun and keep things light and easy.

About the time we started dating, I decided to take shag dance lessons. I asked if he'd like to join me. He did. But we hadn't touched yet, and the teacher kept telling us to hold each other closer, tighter, and look into each other's eyes. It was the most uncomfortable thing! I was laughing on the inside and broke out in a sweat!

There were differences. He often said, "I've never met anyone like you." I remember the shock the night I discovered he was a Republican and his shock realizing I was a Democrat! We talked briefly about it, but basically just laughed. He said he could get along with anybody. It wasn't the deal breaker you'd think.

We continued seeing each other. We talked a lot, and I realized we hadn't kissed and felt it was time. Perhaps exploring the physical realm would help me feel more connected to him.

We were on my couch one evening, and he was about to get up and leave. I gently took his hand. He sat back down, and said, "This is always an awkward thing!"

I'd been with my husband thirty-four years! I'd been single for over a year. Before starting to date again, I couldn't imagine being intimate with another man other than my husband. I might burst into tears, run out of the room, or go frigid when the moment actually occurred.

There I was on the couch with Paul, holding his hand. We kissed, and it was natural. We held each other for a long time and let the kisses linger. His lips were warm.

We got together Monday night, and it was fun in every way. Three nights later was New Year's Eve. As was our style, we usually made plans via text during the week. But the days went by and I didn't hear from him. I was thinking he would suggest something. When I didn't hear, I made quick plans with friends.

At midnight, I texted him a romantic message: "It's midnight, sending a New Year's Eve kiss." I didn't hear back. So I went to bed.

Whenever he read my texts, they would be time stamped on my phone. He didn't read my message until 9:47 a.m. the next day.

I felt the shift. I became teary all morning. After waiting almost four hours, I called him, which I'd never done before. He didn't pick up, and I received an auto-response, "Sorry I can't talk right now."

I called Naomi, who has been single about twenty years. She had become my dating guru. When I told her what happened, she said, "You've been ghosted."

"What is that?" I asked.

"When you're in a relationship with someone and they disappear without saying anything. Like a ghost, they fade away."

I was stunned.

I was fifty-nine and felt like I was fourteen. I was entering a second adolescence. With Paul, I was rediscovering my sexuality and finding new aspects of myself in a new relationship. With the thought of losing him, I felt vulnerable, lost, and confused. I couldn't figure out what I wanted. Could I just let go of Paul?

That night I went to services at my temple. I sat in the back row weeping, letting the music wash over me, soothing me. I wondered, am I this upset over a man I've only known three months? Or is this smaller loss triggering the larger loss, the loss of my husband? Is loss less bearable to me now? Is life simply loss and discovery played over and over?

The next day, Saturday, I wondered what to do. Should I call again? Text or walk away? Ghost him back. No, I couldn't do that. I needed closure.

I wanted to be obvious with my feelings and be a communicator. Either he'll respond or he won't.

On Sunday morning, I decided to text.

My heart raced in the minutes before I sent the text. I typed: "Good Morning, I miss hearing from you! I'm surprised by the turn of events and feel sad and confused. Perhaps there was a misunderstanding? I enjoyed our dates. I'd like to hear from you and see you."

I threw my phone into my purse and zipped it up quickly. I hopped in my car and drove to meet a friend at a coffee shop. When I parked my car, I opened my purse and looked at my phone. He had texted me back immediately.

"New Year's Eve had wiped me out and I've been tying up loose ends ever since," it said.

I detected a little bullshit right there! It had been three days since New Year's Eve.

He added, "Perhaps we can get together later today. Let me know what works best for you."

We decided on getting together for lunch at 1:00 p.m. He offered to pick me up. No, I said, let's meet at an Italian bistro located between where we both lived. When I got there, I saw his car in the parking lot. I walked into the restaurant feeling vulnerable. He was seated at a table and greeted me with a big smile. He jumped up and hugged me. We ate lunch and chatted pleasantly.

After the bill was paid, I said, "I hope it was okay I sent my text."

"Yes, of course. I'm not used to this dating thing. I thought I'd be with one woman my whole life, my wife, but she died. But I met another woman. I'm being honest. I enjoy you both. I'm struggling. It's me, not you."

He repeated that several times: I'm struggling. It's me, not you. His eyes looked red; I think I saw a tear.

There was nervous laughter and talking over each other. After five minutes or so, there wasn't anything else to say. We got up from the table.

I could tell by the way he placed his arm around me as we walked toward the exit that he cared for me. I could tell by the way he walked me to my car across the parking lot and opened my car door, looking and smiling at me the entire time, that he cared for me.

He leaned over and kissed me.

I closed the car door and watched him walk away.

I knew that was our last kiss. I was calm as I drove home. It became clear that the world is imperfect; there are cracks all the way through.

As I pulled into my garage, I repeated, "Julia, you'll be okay, you'll be okay."

Unveiling Ceremony

Unveiling Ceremony, July 26, 2015

Mark Freifeld

Beloved son, brother, husband, father, and grandfather

Psalm 23

The LORD is my shepherd, I shall not be in want.

He makes me lie down in green pastures, he leads me beside quiet waters,

He restores my soul. He guides me in paths of righteousness for his name's sake.

Even though I walk through the valley of the shadow of death, I will fear no evil, for you are with me; your rod and your staff, they comfort me.

You prepare a table before me in the presence of my enemies. You anoint my head with oil, my cup overflows.

Surely goodness and love will follow me all the days of my life, and I will dwell in the house of the LORD forever.

Reading

A smile for all, a heart full of gold

One of the best this world could hold

Never selfish, always kind

A beautiful memory left behind

Kel Maleh Rachamim

אֵל מָלֵא רַחֲמִים שׁוֹכֵן
בַּמְּרוֹמִים הַמְצֵא מְנוּחָה
נְכוֹנָה עַל כַּנְפֵי הַשְּׁכִינָה
בְּמַעֲלוֹת קְדוֹשִׁים וּטְהוֹרִים
כְּזֹהַר הָרָקִיעַ מַזְהִירִים, אֶת
נִשְׁמַת (פלוני בן פלוני)
שֶׁהָלַךְ לְעוֹלָמוֹ,
בַּעֲבוּר שֶׁנָּדְבוּ צְדָקָה
בְּעַד הַזְכָּרַת נִשְׁמָתוֹ, בְּגַן
עֵדֶן תְּהֵא מְנוּחָתוֹ, לָכֵן
בַּעַל הָרַחֲמִים יַסְתִּירֵהוּ
בְּסֵתֶר כְּנָפָיו לְעוֹלָמִים, וְיִצְרֹר
בִּצְרוֹר הַחַיִּים אֶת נִשְׁמָתוֹ,
יְיָ הוּא נַחֲלָתוֹ, וְיָנוּחַ
עַל מִשְׁכָּבוֹ בְּשָׁלוֹם,
וְנֹאמַר אָמֵן:

Ayl mö-lay ra-chamim, sho-chayn
ba-m'romim, ham-tzay m'nuchö
n'chonöh al kan-fey hash-chinöh,
b'ma-alos k'doshim ut'horim
k'zohar hö-röki-a maz-hirim, es
nish-mas (mention his Hebrew name and
that of his father) she-hölach l'olömo,
ba-avur she-nöd'vu tz'dököh
b'ad haz-köras nish-möso, b'gan
ay-den t'hay m'nuchö-so, lö-chayn
ba-al hö-racha-mim yas-tiray-hu
b'sayser k'nöfov l'olö-mim, v'yitz-ror
bitz'ror hacha-yim es nish-möso,
adonöy hu nacha-löso, v'yönu-ach
al mish-kövo b'shölom,
v'no-mar ömayn.

O G-d, full of compassion, Who dwells on high, grant true rest upon the wings of the Shechinah (Divine Presence), in the exalted spheres of the holy and pure, who shine as the resplendence of the firmament, to the soul of Mark (Magid) son of Daniel and Dolores who has gone to his supernal world, for charity has been given in remembrance of his soul; may his place of rest be in Gan Eden. Therefore, may the All-Merciful One shelter him with the cover of His wings forever, and bind his soul in the bond of life. The Everlasting is his heritage; may he rest in his resting-place in peace; and let us say: Amen.

Rooms Remembered

I needed, for months after he died, to remember our rooms—
some lit by the trivial, others ample

with an obscurity that comforted us: it hid our own darkness.
So for months, duteous, I remembered:

rooms where friends lingered, rooms with our beds,
with our books, rooms with curtains I sewed

from bright cottons. I remembered tables of laughter,
a chipped bowl in early light, black

branches by a window, bowing toward night, & those rooms,
too, in which we came together

to be away from all. And sometimes from ourselves:
I remembered that, also.

But tonight—as I stand in the doorway to his room
& stare at dusk settled there—

what I remember best is how, to throw my arms around his neck,
I needed to stand on the tip of my toes.

—Laure-Anne Bosselaar

Mourner's Kaddish

Yis-gadal v'yis-kadash °sh'may rabö°. :יִתְגַּדַּל וְיִתְקַדַּשׁ °שְׁמֵהּ רַבָּא°
(Cong.: Ōmayn.) אמן

B'öl'mö di v'rö chir'u-say בְּעָלְמָא דִּי בְרָא כִרְעוּתֵהּ
v'yam-lich mal'chusay, v'yatz-mach וְיַמְלִיךְ מַלְכוּתֵהּ, וְיַצְמַח
pur-könay °vikö-rayv m'shi-chay°. :פּוּרְקָנֵהּ °וִיקָרֵב מְשִׁיחֵהּ°
(Cong.: Ōmayn.) אמן

B'cha-yay-chon uv'yomay-chon בְּחַיֵּיכוֹן וּבְיוֹמֵיכוֹן
uv'cha-yay d'chöl bays yisrö-ayl, וּבְחַיֵּי דְכָל בֵּית יִשְׂרָאֵל,
ba-agölö uviz'man köriv בַּעֲגָלָא וּבִזְמַן קָרִיב
°v'im'ru ömayn°. (Cong.: Ōmayn. Y'hay וְאִמְרוּ אָמֵן: אמן. יְהֵא שְׁמֵהּ
sh'may rabö m'vörach l'ölam ul'öl'may רַבָּא מְבָרַךְ לְעָלַם וּלְעָלְמֵי
öl'ma-yö. Yisböraych) עָלְמַיָּא: יִתְבָּרֵךְ:

°Y'hay sh'may rabö m'vörach °יְהֵא שְׁמֵהּ רַבָּא מְבָרַךְ
l'ölam ul'öl'may öl'ma-yö. :לְעָלַם וּלְעָלְמֵי עָלְמַיָּא
Yis-böraych° °v'yish-tabach, יִתְבָּרֵךְ° °וְיִשְׁתַּבַּח,
v'yispö-ayr, v'yis-romöm, וְיִתְפָּאַר, וְיִתְרוֹמַם,
v'yis-nasay, v'yis-hadör, וְיִתְנַשֵּׂא, וְיִתְהַדָּר,
v'yis-aleh, v'yis-halöl°, °sh'may וְיִתְעַלֶּה, וְיִתְהַלָּל°, °שְׁמֵהּ
d'kud-shö b'rich hu°. :דְּקֻדְשָׁא בְּרִיךְ הוּא°
(Cong.: Ōmayn.) אמן

L'aylö min köl bir'chösö v'shi-rösö, לְעֵלָּא מִן כָּל בִּרְכָתָא וְשִׁירָתָא,
tush-b'chösö v'neche-mösö, תֻּשְׁבְּחָתָא וְנֶחֱמָתָא,
da-amirön b'öl'mö, דַּאֲמִירָן בְּעָלְמָא,
°v'im'ru ömayn°. :וְאִמְרוּ אָמֵן°
(Cong.: Ōmayn.) אמן

Y'hay sh'lömö rabö min sh'ma-yö, יְהֵא שְׁלָמָא רַבָּא מִן שְׁמַיָּא
v'cha-yim tovim ölay-nu v'al köl וְחַיִּים טוֹבִים עָלֵינוּ וְעַל כָּל
yisrö-ayl °v'im'ru ömayn°. :יִשְׂרָאֵל °וְאִמְרוּ אָמֵן°
(Cong.: Ōmayn.) אמן

Take three steps back and say the following, while bowing the head
to the right, straight ahead, left, straight ahead, and bowing down (as indicated):

> Oseh shölom* bim'romöv, ^ hu > עֹשֶׂה שָׁלוֹם* בִּמְרוֹמָיו, ^ הוּא
< ya-aseh shölom ölaynu, ^ v'al köl < יַעֲשֶׂה שָׁלוֹם עָלֵינוּ, ^ וְעַל כָּל
yisrö-ayl, °v'im'ru ömayn°. :יִשְׂרָאֵל, °וְאִמְרוּ אָמֵן°
(Cong.: Ōmayn.) אמן

Exalted and hallowed be God's great name
in the world which God created, according to plan.
May God's majesty be revealed in the days of our lifetime
and the life of all Israel — speedily, imminently,
To which we say: Amen.
Blessed be God's great name to all eternity.
Blessed, praised, honored, exalted,
extolled, glorified, adored, and lauded
be the name of the Holy Blessed One,
beyond all earthly words and songs of blessing, praise, and comfort.
To which we say: Amen.

May there be abundant peace from heaven, and life, for us
and all Israel.
To which we say: Amen.
May the One who creates harmony on high, bring peace to us
and to all Israel.
To which we say: Amen.

If by Chance

If by chance, you have a
memory of me,
Let it be one of laughter;
Let me leave to you
a memory of joy.

And if, by chance, you have a
thought of me,
Let it be one of understanding;
Let me leave with you
companionship in sorrow.

And, when, by chance,
you dream of me,
Let it be one of love;
Let the memory of my love
be your greatest gift of all.

—Author Unknown

Resources

Transitions LifeCare Caregiver Support Center
3724 National Drive
Raleigh, NC 27612
www.guidinglightsnc.org

Lotsa Helping Hands: Care for the Caregiver
www.lotsahelpinghands.com

Mark Freifeld Memorial Research Fund
MSA Research Fundraising
www.markfreifeld.com

Mayo Clinic
Locations in Minnesota,
Florida, and Arizona
www.mayoclinic.org

The MSA Coalition
Support • Education • Research • Advocacy
www.multiplesystematrophy.org
MSA has multiple Facebook pages where you can get additional information regarding support groups and so forth.

National Organization for Rare Disorders
55 Kenosia Avenue
Danbury, CT 06810
www.rarediseases.org

Reflections: A Memoir
Mark Freifeld

Caregivers Summit
Respite * Resolution * Resources
A yearly conference with
multiple locations
www.caregiverssummit.org

Transitions LifeCare
250 Hospice Circle
Raleigh, NC 27607
www.transitionslifecare.org

Vanderbilt Autonomic Dysfunction Center
Vanderbilt University Medical Center
1211 Medical Center Drive
Nashville, TN 37232
https://www.vumc.org/autonomic-dysfunction-center/vanderbilt-
autonomic-dysfunction

Well Spouse Association
63 West Main Street Suite H
Freehold, NJ 07728
www.wellspouse.org

Mobility Aids and Equipment

To stay ahead of Mark's needs, we were constantly researching products to help Mark and bring comfort to him. Here's a list of mobility aids and equipment we found useful:

- Pill crusher (for when Mark could no longer swallow pills whole)

- 3-in-1 vehicle support handle (a safety tool that helped Mark get in and out of his car; it slid into the car door latch)

- Rubber band hand exerciser (builds hand strength with light resistance)

- EZ Reacher (26-inch aid provided help to grasp hard-to-reach items)

- 24-inch-handle shoehorn (helped Mark slip into shoes with limited range of motion)

- Stander bed cane with organizer (provides extra support in getting in and out of bed; the pouch was for keeping items close by)

- Wood cane with contour handle (this had the right feel in Mark's hand and helped him balance while walking)

- Compression socks (knee-high stockings to help with poor circulation)

- Suction aspirator (for oral suction)

- Stander Assist-a-tray (tray has a handle that made standing and sitting easy and safe; the swivel tray pivots away when not in use)

- Food blender (we went through three blenders preparing meals for Mark)

- Gait belt (a device worn around the waist to transfer Mark from one position to another)

- Grab bars for bathrooms and hallways (to assist Mark and prevent falls)

- DynaVox (touch screen and eye control communication device)

- Portable threshold ramp (aluminum lightweight folding ramp for wheelchairs and scooters)

- Folding walker (lightweight aluminum)

- 4-wheel walker (this is a walker and chair combo for indoor and outdoor use)

- Stair lift (mechanical device for lifting people up and down stairs)

- Lift chair recliner (electric chair with multiple positions for seating, sleeping, and lifting people to almost standing)

- Hoyer lift (a sit-to-stand patient lift)

- Travel wheelchair (lightweight and foldable)

- Electric scooter (battery-operated wheelchair)

- Power wheelchair with elevating leg rest with calf pads

- Geo-Matt Therapeutic Overlay (an aid in the prevention and treatment of pressure sores that enhances circulation, channeling heat away from the patient to minimize perspiration buildup)

- Hospital bed (adjustable height for entire bed, plus the head, feet, and side rails)

- Tempur-Pedic bed (This was similar to a hospital bed but much more comfortable. We bought two twins and placed them side by side. Mark could be propped up and I could be lying flat. Its height was not adjustable.)

- Accessible van (allowing Mark to travel by vehicle in a wheelchair)

- Wooden ramps built over doorjambs and from kitchen to garage to accommodate the scooter and wheelchairs

- Plastic shelving for medicines and supplies by his bed

Things we had to take out of our home:

- The area rugs in the kitchen and the mats in the bathrooms because they would get caught in the wheelchair wheels

- We moved furniture to make passageways to accommodate the wheelchair

Acknowledgments

AS IN THE SHAMANIC RITUAL of circling the room and bringing in everything that is life-affirming, I want to thank the people who made my book possible. Above all, I want to thank my family and friends who held my hand, talked, and walked the walk with me as I helplessly watched Mark succumb to his horrendous disease. Your caring and generous friendship will never be forgotten.

To Carrie Knowles—if it were not for your steady presence and editing skills, my private journal entries would never have made it to manuscript. You pushed me to go deeper and examine feelings more fully, and I am thankful.

Thank you to Brenda Herrmann and Ellen Levine, who read early drafts; your valuable comments and encouragement kept me going. Thank you to Laurie Evans and to James and Emily Kotecki—editors extraordinaire!

In addition to thanking the family and friends mentioned in my book, I'd like to extend appreciation to dearest friends who surrounded Mark, my family, and me with love: Joyce, Anya, Arthur, Margaret, Ossie, Jackie, Michael, Alan, Steve, Janice, Matt, Shelly, Chip, Leigh, Ash, Dick, Jeff, Loretta, Avi, Rebecca, two Nancys, three Cindys, Joel, Jennifer, Deirdre, Jill, Helen, Kent, Emily O., Fil, Robyn, Page, Sona, Bob, Celeste, Scott, Adrienne, and Kelly.

Rabbi Lucy Dinner's comforting discussions with Mark and me in our home, leading of the funeral, and guidance after Mark's passing are deeply appreciated.

Mark's hospice team was assigned randomly, but the relationships between us grew and seemed meant to be. Thank you for your support and wisdom.

The CNAs really were our team of angels. Our days were made easier by your presence.

To the doctors and staff, especially Dr. Phillip Low and Dr. Paola Sandroni at Mayo Clinic in Rochester, Minnesota: I'm thankful for your expertise, professionalism, and continued dedication to this rare disease. Without Dr. Ana Felix, we'd never have thought to go to Mayo Clinic; my gratitude. Mark's primary care physician was Dr. James Jacobs; his sage advice helped us navigate Mark's illness. For her kind visits to our home once treatments were no longer effective, Dr. Rhonda Gabr, one of Mark's neurologists, will always be remembered. Thank you.

Lives aren't lived one story at a time. Before Mark's diagnosis, my mother, Barbara Leve, began showing signs of Alzheimer's disease. Her slow descent into that disease and the caregiving journey of my father, Jerry Leve, was concurrent with Mark's and my family's experience.

Eventually my parents moved to Charlotte to live near my sister, Caren Gale, and her husband, Charlie Gale. Caren and Charlie shouldered dual responsibility of helping our parents, and I thank them for their loving and attentive care.

Poetry was my mother's artistic expression. A special thank you to her for opening the world of poetry to me.

Thank you to my daughters-in-law, Jennifer and Elena Freifeld, and son-in-law, James Kotecki, for their insight, love, and care.

To my late mother-in-law, Dolores Freifeld, and dearest children, Jeremy Freifeld, Emily Kotecki, and David Freifeld, thank you for allowing our family's most poignant tragedy to be shared and trusting me to tell our story.